THE LIFE AND TIMES OF DENIS JULIEN

FUR TRADER

THE LIFE AND TIMES OF DENIS JULIEN

FUR TRADER

By
James H. Knipmeyer

Front cover photo: Denis Julien, Devils Garden.
Oil painting by Pete Plastow, Moab, Utah.
Back cover photo: Author photo by Mike Ford.

© 2018, James H. Knipmeyer
First Edition

Without limiting the rights under copyright reserved above, no part of this publication may be reproduced, stored in or introduced into a retrieval system, or transmitted, in any form or by any means (electronic, mechanical, photocopying, recording, or otherwise), without the prior written permission of both the copyright owner and the publisher of this book.

Published by Aventine Press
55 E. Emerson St.
Chula Vista CA, 91911

ISBN: 978-1-59330-948-0

Printed in the United States of America
ALL RIGHTS RESERVED

TABLE OF CONTENTS

Ouverture		7
One:	Le Mystérieux D. Julien	13
Two:	Les Rapides des Moines	23
Three:	L'Entrepreneur	35
Four:	Ami ou Ennemi	47
Five:	Le Litigateur	59
Six:	Prairie du Chien	67
Seven:	La Rivière Platte	75
Eight:	La Provincia de Nuevo México	81
Nine:	El Plateau Colorado	89
Ten:	Uinta-ats Revenge	101
Dénouement		107
Endnotes		111
Bibliography		119

OUVERTURE

The rising sun was just peeking through the silhouetted foliage of the willow and sycamore trees which lined the far distant Illinois shore. Fading tendrils of morning mist still curled slowly upward from the broad, turgid expanse of the Mississippi River. Along the near bank the cool air of the already busy St. Louis waterfront hummed and roared with a babel of French, Spanish, and English voices and shouts. The squealing wagons of draymen, with their braying mules or bellowing oxen, carted bales, boxes, and crates of various cargo and goods down to the shoreline. There they were hefted and hoisted by stevedores of white, black, and brown color onto the waiting decks and into the dim-lit holds of the queue of keelboats, barges, and *bateaus* that were crowded closely together gunwale to gunwale.

On this morning of March 22, 1798, the linen broadcloth-clad figure of François Cailhol hastily made his way up the slanting gangplank from the rocky levee and on board the *galion La Flètch*. Already loaded and ready to shove off, mooring lines were untied, poles pushed into the shallow water, and the gunboat slowly edged away from the shore. Angled across smoothly roiling eddies and into the sluggish, but powerful current, the vessel began to laboriously make its way upstream, gradually leaving the feverish activity and raucous noise in its wake. Cailhol was an interpreter and pilot, and though like him the boat too bore a French name, the actual command of the vessel was under the smartly uniformed and Spanish-bred Don Bernardo Molina.

The village of St. Louis had been founded in 1764 by New Orleans trader Pierre Laclède Liguest and his stepson, Auguste Chouteau. The settlement was built on a gently sloping hillside that rose up from a low limestone bluff on the west bank of the Mississippi, a half-dozen miles below the mouth of the muddy Missouri River. By the latter part of the 1700s, because of its geographical location and the natural mooring possibilities of its rocky bluff, the town had emerged as the focal point of commerce and population in Upper Louisiana.

At this time, some thirty-five years after the conclusion of what in North America became known as the French and Indian War, all of Louisiana, the vast tract of land that stretched from the banks of the Mississippi River west as far as the crests of the Stoney, or Rocky Mountains, belonged to Spain, having been secretly ceded from France in 1762. Since the Treaty of Paris in 1763, the new Spanish administration had relied heavily on the former French officials and Gallic populous to assist in both governing the territory and maintaining its trade relations with the Native American tribes. Except for a small number of Spanish officials and soldiers, during the ensuing four decades not more than a dozen Spaniards had actually settled in the St. Louis area. Louisiana remained thoroughly French in population, language, customs, and outlook.

The task of *Capitán* Molina and the handful of other Spanish gunboats was to patrol the watery miles of the Mississippi River, particularly above St. Louis, or as it was presently known, San Luis. They were to be watchful of any Indian unrest from the interior and, just as importantly, be on the lookout for any British movements and possible incursions from the north. This particular patrol of March, 1798, plied its way upriver to the north, its goal the village of Prairie du Chien just above the mouth of the Ouisconsin River. There Cailhol owned property and resided.

The name Mississippi was the French rendering of the Native American Ojibway title *Misi-ziibi*, meaning "Great River." The Spanish gunboat, its name of "The Arrow" notwithstanding, had a slow and arduous time making headway upstream against the strong current, even utilizing both oars, sail, and the occasional *cordelle* – the use of tow-ropes from the shore. Therefore it was seventeen days later, on April 8, that the *La Fletch*, now some 250 miles from St. Louis, between the mouths of the Iowa and Rock Rivers, met a canoe being swiftly paddled downstream and manned by six men.

In his semi-daily and often misspelled journal, which Cailhol kept as a form of report for the Spanish *comandante* in San Luis, he proceeded to put name to each of the six canoeists, either for official purposes or, more likely, because he was personally acquainted with and knew all of them. Cailhol listed "Louis Honnorest [sic], Father and Son,

... old Dorrion [sic] and his nephew Collte [sic], *Denis Julien* and La Liberté...."[1] [Author's emphasis]

The two passing groups camped together that night, before each going their opposite ways the following morning. Just what these six men were doing on their downstream voyage, and key to the story of Denis Julien, was briefly mentioned by Cailhol in his April 8 journal entry: "On this day we met... their bark canoe *loaded with furs*." [Author's emphasis] Succinctly put, Denis Julien was a fur trader.

* * *

It was in 1535 that Jacques Cartier first sailed up what he named *Le Rivière Saint Laurens,* the St. Lawrence River, and took possession of all of the surrounding lands for France. The areas that lay alongside that stream came to be called Canada, from the Native American Iroquois word for "village" or "settlement." The first Europeans to enter the northeastern region of the North American continent, like Cartier, came in search of the elusive Northwest Passage, that mythical trade route to the riches of the Orient. However, it did not take long for these early French explorers to realize there was no such westward-leading strait of water. Neither was there any obvious mineral wealth in the form of precious metals, which had been discovered and diligently searched for by the competing Spanish *conquistadores* far to the southwest. But they did find what would prove to be riches of another sort – the land's abundant animal furs, which came to be referred to as "soft gold."

In 1603 a fur trade monopoly was granted by the French king for the region by then known as *Nouvelle France*, and just a few years later the town of Québec was founded by Samuel de Champlain. This was followed in 1611 by the establishment of a fur trading station further up the St. Lawrence River near the head of practical navigation for large ocean-going vessels. This small post would, in the years ahead, become the future town of Montréal. These inroads marked the beginning of the westward movement of French fur traders up the St. Lawrence River and into the *Pays du Haut*, the "Upper Country," around the Great Lakes.

By 1642 the now "town" of Montréal had become the fur trade center of the surrounding region, and in 1660 *Nouvelle France* became the Royal Province of New France. All of this growth was due to the burgeoning fur trade, and among the many animals sought for their pelts, *les castors*, the beaver, were at the forefront. The reason was relatively simple.

In the mid-1600s only a comparative few European men worked as merchants in shops. Most males spent their days out of doors, farming or transporting goods from one place to another. This of course was done no matter what the weather and whatever the season, and centuries of experience had shown that the most useful item to have in inclement weather was good, protective headgear. And the best hats, it was found, were made from beaver. Their fur could be worked into a pliable felt, which could then be formed by hatters into a finished product that would keep the wearer both dry and warm.

The beaver pelts were actually sought out for their wooly underfur. Each soft hair had tiny barbs which held them tightly together and made this underfur very dense and, therefore, nearly waterproof. This was the raw material for the resulting felt that went into the making of many different types of hats. By the end of the Middle Ages hats were one way to distinguish one class from another, and even what trade or profession a person might be engaged in. The resulting styles, in various shapes and colors, were worn by everyone from common laborers to upper-class gentlemen.

Throughout Europe such hats had traditionally come from the fur of the European beaver, found in the northern regions such as Scandinavia and Russia. However, over-hunting had nearly depleted the beaver population by the time of the establishment of the new European colonies in North America during the 1500s. Therefore, the market for the American beaver was both immense and, therefore, very profitable. The heyday of this new fur trade would last for the next two and a half centuries, and would also encompass the life of Denis Julien.

St. Louis, late 1700s.
Frederic L. Billon, *Annals of St. Louis*
St. Louis: privately printed, 1886.

ONE

LE MYSTÉRIEUX D. JULIEN

"The Mysterious D. Julien." Thus did Denis Julien's first biographer refer to him.[1] "Mysterious" because little could be learned of the life of this man: where he was born, his movements and travels across the country, not even when or where he died. However, because, as Monsieur Cailhol indicated, Julien was a trader in furs, a study of the background of that industry in North America can provide valuable clues as to his probable origin.

By the mid-seventeenth century there was only a score of permanent settlers in Québec, who in turn were greatly outnumbered by the transient fur traders. Also by that time, in an average year as many as fifteen to twenty thousand furs, mostly those of beaver, were being shipped to France. However, during the middle part of the 1600s the Native American tribe known as the Iroquois had effectively blockaded the upper St. Lawrence River and direct access to the Great Lakes region. At this time the only people who could achieve any success in the fur trade were those who knew the land just as well as the Indians did and could live and survive in the backwoods for months at a time. Therefore, a group of predominantly young men, who had learned the ways of the wilderness from the natives themselves, became the mainstays of the fur trade. These adventurers came to be known as *coureurs des bois*, or literally "woods runners."

Most of these individuals had been born in New France and a good number often spent the summers clearing and farming plots of land adjacent to the St. Lawrence River. But in the fall they would travel upriver and inland to the Huron and Ojibway villages, where they passed the winter trading for furs. When the rivers and streams cleared of ice in the spring, they would smuggle their accumulated furs through the Iroquois and back to Montréal or Québec.

For the most part the woods runners, with a few exceptions obviously, could neither read nor write. They were usually of such a low social status that they could not obtain official trading licenses from the colonial government, which favored people who had wealth and education or connections to the French crown. The licenses required fees to be paid to the government, as well as a percentage of the traders' subsequent profits. The woods runners ignored the rules and the licenses, left the farmland the government wanted them to work, and sought their fortunes in the wilderness. This illegal trade began to flourish because no one else had the survival skills or knew the native languages well enough to be equally as successful.

In 1665, after the French had succeeded, temporarily at least, in destroying the hostile grip of the Iroquois alliance along the St. Lawrence River, scores of Frenchmen from Montréal and Québec sought to gain a share of the potential profits to be had and traveled west with the flotilla of Indian traders to the Great Lakes region and Michilimackinac. First visited some three decades earlier by Jean Nicolet, Michilimackinac was the phonetic French spelling of the Native American Ojibway name *mi-shine-mack na-go*, meaning "large turtle." This title referred to the shape of what has since become known simply as Mackinac Island. It is located in the narrow strait of water separating Lakes Huron and Michigan, and not far west of the short connection northward to Lake Superior. Thus it had always been a vital crux point in the fur trade of the surrounding region.

In 1673, Father Jacques Marquette and fur trader Louis Jolliet left Michilimackinac, made their way southwest, eventually reaching the Mississippi River. This stream they ultimately descended as far south as the mouth of today's Arkansas River. After he had established the first trading station at Michilimackinac six years later, René Robert Cavelier, Sieur de la Salle, in 1682 followed the length of the Mississippi to near the Gulf and claimed all of the land it drained for France. He gave it the name *Louisiane*, after King Louis XIV. That name, usually spelled Louisiana, came to be used, however, principally for the lands lying on the west side of the Mississippi. Those to the east became known as the *Pays des Illinois*, or "Illinois Country," after a Native American tribe of that name who lived in the region.

Subsequently, scores of boatmen, known as *voyageurs*, and traders traveled from Michilimackinac, southward to the Illinois Country. For various reasons most of the men that operated out of Michilimackinac turned south toward the upper Mississippi region rather than northwest into the Canadian interior. Potential Native American customers were more numerous in the south, and the winters, prime time for fur gathering, were less severe. Moreover, the Canadian tribes proved to be more and more intractable and unpredictable.

The French fur men soon found that to the Native Americans, while there was no ownership in the European sense of the land itself, each tribe did have what amounted to property rights of the game animals that roamed within certain definable boundaries. Therefore, the early fur men did little or no hunting or trapping themselves, but acquired the pelts and hides they desired directly from the natives by way of trade. The inducements that they used were European manufactured goods that seemed to promise an easier way of surmounting the often harsh surroundings: a musket or trade rifle for hunting for the men, and metal pots and other cooking utensils for the women. Habit soon turned these luxuries into necessities.

The pelts gathered by the Indians were usually taken during the winter season, when the animal's fur was at its prime as far as luster and thickness were concerned. The traders soon learned that the Indians were reluctant to travel the long distance to an established trading post such as Michilimackinac, as this would have often taken members of the more distant tribes through the intervening lands of unfriendly neighbors. Therefore, the enterprising trader quickly found that it was more to his advantage to actually go to the villages and hunting areas himself to acquire the furs, rather than to sit back and wait for the Indian hunters to bring them to him. Through discreet persuasion and the providing of a few trade goods on credit, he could keep them purposefully at work throughout the winter. The lifestyle of the earlier *coureur de bois* was back in vogue once again.

During the remainder of the 1600s and the first half of the 1700s, the flow of European trade goods in exchange for native furs steadily increased. By the mid-1700s the vast majority of Native American men, not only in the Great Lakes region but now in the upper Mississippi area also, wore at least some clothing of European manufacture, as well as woolen blankets, rather than tanned leather or fur. Trade goods, besides guns and metal kettles, now included such items as iron hatchets, fishhooks, ice chisels, awls, knives, lead shot, and gunpowder. There were also the so-called luxury items like needles, glass beads, brooches, armbands, earbobs, ribbons, copper bells, combs, mirrors, tobacco, and liquor, such as brandy, rum, and whiskey.

The fur trade also affected how the Native American tribes conducted their seasonal rounds of living. In summer they usually lived in large, semi-permanent villages, which often consisted of several hundred people. At this time they fished, gathered nuts and berries, grew crops for food, and hunted small game animals. In the winter a good portion of the men would split up into bands for the hunting of the larger game animals in more distant places. As the fur trade became more important to them, the natives began their winter hunts earlier and traveled farther away from their home villages. They also focused more and more on hunting those animals that produced valuable pelts, rather than concentrating on those killed solely for their meat and hides.

Besides the individual *coureurs de bois*, furs were also obtained by the larger trading companies that sent out *engagés*, or employees, in small groups, though more often individually, to trade with the Indians *en la dérouine*. This was a French term original to the fur trade with no English equivalent. In general it referred to trade with the natives on their own grounds, away from the trading stations. These small groups and individuals went out in search of native bands, established contact with them, and routinely stayed for prolonged periods of time. They soon learned that they became closer to the Indians, with resulting better trade options, when they actually lived and worked with them through the winter season. During these *sojournés*, they traded with the native peoples directly at their villages.

These traders, now known as *hivernants*, or "winterers," also found that they had even better luck in their trade endeavors when they could utilize familial contacts. Many of them integrated themselves into the native society through marriage, further strengthening economic ties. This seems to have been the case with Denis Julien.

* * *

When Julien and his companions separated from Cailhol and his party on the morning of April 9, 1798, they continued to paddle on downstream, aided by the swift current of the mighty Mississippi. In just six days they had arrived in St. Louis, and there is found the first written signature of Julien himself. It is at the bottom of the baptismal record for his daughter, and much can be gleaned and inferred from this document concerning his earlier life.

In essence the brief entry states that on April 15, 1798, the rite of baptism was performed at the Catholic Church of St. Louis for Marie Josephe, born on May 5, 1793, and the illegitimate daughter of Denis Julien and Catherine, Indian, of the Ayouiz [sic] Nation.[2]

Based on the birthdate of who would seem to be his oldest child, Denis Julien himself was probably born sometime between 1771 and 1775, and thus in 1798 would have been somewhere from 22 to 26 years of age. He had a Native American wife, a member of the Ioway tribe, but had not been "legally" married to her under the rites and sacraments of the Catholic Church. Brief, but telling.

Perhaps the most important fact contained in this baptismal record is the length of time between the birth of Marie Josephe and her later baptism – some five years. The Catholic doctrine on the necessity of baptism for salvation of the soul has not changed since the early centuries of the Church. The Catechism teaches that only through baptism can a person be freed from original sin. Therefore, canon law states that parents are obligated to see that their children are baptized within the first few weeks after their birth. Devout Catholic parents, then, would want to have their newborn children baptized as soon as possible. This, obviously, Denis Julien did not do, and there was probably a combination of reasons why.

In 1798 there was only one functioning church in the entire upper Mississippi region. Though there had been a Catholic mission on Mackinac Island since the late 1660s, after 1765 there was no resident priest assigned there until 1830. Likewise, in the French trading town of Prairie du Chien, on the upper Mississippi, a Catholic church was not even organized until the early 1820s. That left the town of St. Louis, which did in fact have a Catholic church, the Church of the Parish of

St. Louis, originally established in 1770. From 1794 until 1799, Dom Pierre Didier served as parish priest, but, perhaps significantly, was not in residency full-time.

Also, there was the probable location of Julien's and his family's home. The first French traders had reached the Native American Ioway tribe by 1677, just a few years on the heels of Marquette's and Joliet's voyage down the Mississippi River. Their own name for themselves was *Báxoje*, "Gray Snow" or "Dusted Faces." The Lakota Sioux version of this name was *Ayúxba* which in the French transliteration became *Aiouez*. In English it was finally rendered as Ioway, or Iowa. In 1798 separate bands of the tribe lived in villages on both the present-day Iowa and Des Moines Rivers in the modern state of Iowa. It was in this east-central Iowa area that Julien and his family probably lived, very likely with or nearby his wife's family, far from the nearest Catholic church.

It is informative to note that while the "Report of the Archivist of the Province of Quebec" includes trade contracts, names of traders and boatmen, and the destinations of all parties outfitted for the Indian trade granted by the British-Canadian government in Québec and Montréal from 1768 until 1790, none were to or of Denis Julien. It seems probable, then, that he carried on the same lifestyle as the early French *coureur de bois*, who had now evolved into what was known as the free, or independent, trader. This man hired himself out to no company, but was his own master, going where he pleased, when he pleased, and with all the fruits of his labor being entirely his own. He sought some native encampment or village, took up his home there, and spent the greater part of the year in the wilderness. Only once in a while would he come in touch with the civilized world, when he brought his furs out to market. He cared little where or to whom he sold his peltries, so long as he was fairly paid.

In Julien's case, when the winter snows began to melt and the spring thaw began breaking up the ice in the streams, he may often have simply brought his season's or year's accumulation of furs to the bank of the Mississippi. There he would eventually hail a passing canoe or *bateau*, give them his *piéces*, or packs, of pelts to transport, perhaps on consignment, either north to Prairie du Chien and on to Mackinac, or south to St. Louis. Later, on their return, the *voyageurs* could easily have dropped off supplies and trade goods to Julien for the coming year.

These independent traders, like Julien, were typically considered social outcasts and were a constant source of worry and frustration to the Spanish authorities in St. Louis. Like the French and later British in Canada, trading in Upper Louisiana was theoretically open to any Spanish subject. Traders were, however, supposed to acquire licenses from the Spanish lieutenant-governor. But also like the earlier regimes, these often went to the highest, and therefore wealthiest, bidders, effectively shutting out the small free traders. Therefore, Julien and his like often ignored such permits. They were also troublesome to both the Spanish government and the large, established merchant-traders in yet another way. Having significant influence with the Native American tribes because of their long affiliations and blood-kin ties, these free traders could give partisan counsel to the tribes they were now a part of and sometimes go against official Spanish interests.

For any or all of these reasons, then, Julien may himself simply not gone downriver to St. Louis very often. He may have felt a distinct lack of welcome there for his "kind."

While all of this does give some knowledge of Julien's probable physical whereabouts and doings during this period in his life, his relationship with his wife Catherine provides us with a more intimate insight into his feelings, personality, and temperament.

While many of the French "winterers" took on a Native American female as a "night woman" on only a seasonal basis, it was not all that uncommon for some to establish a more permanent alliance. This was a relatively uncomplicated affair. The trader simply asked for the consent of the woman's father, brother, or other family head, followed by the payment of a "bride price." This was most often in the form of trade goods. Such couples regarded themselves as married, and the husband and wife were expected to remain loyal to each other.

More than just providing a sexual companionship, native wives were often critical to their trader-husband's success. They served as interpreters and guides, prepared meals, helped dress furs for shipment, and managed the camps that the traders used as a home during their sojourns into the wilderness. These unions created strong bonds between the traders and their wives' tribes or bands, and made for a much smoother trading relationship.

Such tribal "marriages" came to be known as *mariage á la façon du pays*, or "marriage in the custom of the country." Most of the French traders involved took them seriously, with the unions lasting many years and producing multiple children. Families became even more important for those traders, such as Denis Julien, who decided not to leave the interior and settled down with their Native American wives in or close to their home villages. Julien and others like him looked upon these unions to be just as respected and permanent as church ceremonies.

* * *

Denis Julien, however, does continue to be "mysterious" in at least one very important regard – his place of birth. A Julien namesake, formerly of Detroit, Michigan, after hearing his story spent several years and traveled many miles during the 1960s and 1970s in an attempt to establish a familial connection between Denis and himself. This, of course, also entailed trying to find a birthplace and possible ancestry. A subsequent exhaustive and thorough search of the Canadian archives, both those of the government and those in historical and trade society records, unfortunately, proved futile. It was as if Julien arrived on the scene in 1798 "fully formed" and with no apparent background other than having a Native American wife and child.

However, Julien's intimate association with the Ioway tribe, historically more closely allied to the British-Canadians to the north rather than the St. Louis and Louisiana French to the south; his future business and commercial contacts with Mackinac on the Great Lakes; and the fact that in later years he was at least a temporary resident of Prairie du Chien, north in what is now Wisconsin; would all seem to point to probable familial connections in French Canada. Denis Julien, until new, concrete evidence is discovered in some dusty, hidden ledger or record book, was most likely a *Québécois*, a French-Canadian of the upper St. Lawrence country. He was probably of "low" birth or social class, who at an early age "took off" for the fur country to the west. He aligned himself with no trading company and, like other *coureurs des bois*, went his own way to seek his fortune.

St. Louis catholic church, 1776.
Rev. John Rothensteiner, *History of the Archdiocese of St. Louis*
St. Louis, Missouri: Blackwell Wielandy Co., 1928.

TWO
LES RAPIDES DES MOINES

Denis Julien was born into a world of political upheaval. A decade earlier France and Great Britain had been embroiled in the so-called Seven Years War, which had rippled its way across the waters of the Atlantic to those two countries' New World possessions. Here it became known as the French and Indian War. Though the conflict did not officially come to an end until 1763, for all practical purposes it was over in North America by 1759. In that year, on the *Plaines d'Abraham* outside of Québec, the French forces under Louis Joseph, Marquis de Montcalm, were defeated by the British army under the command of General James Wolfe.

Three years later, when defeat became apparent in Europe as well, the clandestine Treaty of Fontainebleau was concluded in 1762. To thwart Britain from gaining control of all France's North American possessions, Louisiana, west of the Mississippi River, was secretly ceded to Spain. Subsequently, with the official Treaty of Paris ending the war the following year, Great Britain took control of all of what had been New France in the St. Lawrence-Great Lakes region and the Illinois Country east of the Mississippi.

As with the Spanish in Louisiana, the British rule of the St. Lawrence, Great Lakes, and Illinois was more superficial than deeply rooted. Especially in the predominant industry of the fur trade, while the new owners and directors may now have been English, the everyday working subaltern supervisors and clerks were, more often than not, retained Frenchmen. And while British adventurers more and more entered into the ranks of the actual men in the field, the *engagés*, *voyageurs*, and *sojourneurs*, the majority were still of French-Canadian linage.

Such political turmoil continued even in the years immediately after Julien's birth, when open conflict developed between England and her American colonies along the Atlantic seaboard. With the exception of General George Rogers Clark's surprise captures of the British garrisons at Vincennes on the Wabash River and Kaskaskia on the Illinois side of the Mississippi, most of the battles and fighting took place farther to the east. Ultimately, however, a new Treaty of Paris, this in the fall of 1783, proclaimed American victory and independence from Great Britain. It also foreshadowed the formation of a new country, which now extended westward as far as the east bank of the Mississippi River. But in the years after the Revolutionary War, United States rule was much like that of Britain after the French and Indian War – superficial and shallowly rooted. Everyday life, including that of the fur traders, remained predominantly in the hands of the French and their English overseers.

* * *

During the American Revolution the British trading firms operating out of Canada had drastically curtailed their activities in what was to become United States territory. This created an economic opportunity for the smaller, independent traders, who had no binding allegiance to England or the new infant country.

When Julien finally left his home for the fur trade to the west and southwest, he had several choices of tribes into which he could insinuate himself. There were the *Ho-Chunk*, or Winnebago, in what is now north-central Wisconsin; the *Meskwaki*, called by the French the Fox, in southern Wisconsin; the *Oakiwaki*, known as the Sauk to the French, in northern Illinois; the *Nadouessioux*, more commonly referred to simply as the Sioux, in southwestern Minnesota; and the *Báxoje*, the Ioway, in today's state of that name.

British, and now American, authority encompassed the tribal territories of the Winnebago, Fox, and Sauk peoples. Therefore, since Julien and the other independent traders did not desire or want to be under the yoke of governmental regulations, those tribes were passed by. The Ioways, on the other hand, lived on the west side of the Mississippi, outside of American control, and were in a nearly direct line with the long-used French trading route from Green Bay, on Lake Michigan, southwest along the Fox and Wisconsin River waterways to the Mississippi.

Though now nominally under the control of the Spanish, the Ioways for well over a century had been in contact with French traders from the north. Even after British, and now American, takeover, the tribe still looked predominantly in that direction for their trading. The fur trade on the west bank of the upper Mississippi, above St. Louis, remained firmly under the influence of the British from Michilimackinac and Prairie du Chien. The inability of Spanish, and now American, merchants to provide enough goods for this trade in effect forced all of the upper Mississippi tribes, not just the Ioways, to turn primarily to the well-supplied British traders. The English not only provided superior trade goods, but they also paid higher prices for pelts, since England had now become Europe's leading furrier.

Therefore, at the beginning of the nineteenth century the Ioways, while still living in the Spanish sphere of influence, were not under the thumb of its government and were able to maintain their tribal sovereignty. Though keeping their long-established trade relations with the British of the Great Lakes region, they continued to maintain diplomatic ties with Spanish St. Louis. During this time the tribal leaders became very adept in playing one side off against the other.

A document dated for the first of April, 1800, was written and signed by Denis Julien, evidently for the Spanish officials in St. Louis. Referred to as a "passport," it is a voucher, or safe-conduct pass, for an Indian named "Masacaé." In it Julien certified that the Ioway was the son of a chief, and described him as having good intentions toward the Spanish government.[1] This document, then, clearly shows that, even at this early time, Julien was already a significant *liaison* between the Native Americans and the whites.

Perhaps just as importantly, however, at least as far as Julien's earlier upbringing is concerned, is the fact that he wrote out and signed the passport himself. The simple fact of his being able to write, and even the penmanship itself, would seem to indicate at least a basic education of some sort during his formative years.

Denis Julien must also have had some exposure to the Catholic religion in his younger life. His name now began to appear on an occasional basis in the baptismal records of the St. Louis church. In them was recorded the birth of a son, Etienne, in early 1799. However, similar to what transpired with his older sister, the baptism did not take place until 1804.[2] A second son, Pierre Paschal, however, who was born in April of 1800, was baptized just a year and a half later, in October of 1801.[3] It is somewhat strange that the younger son would have been baptized some three years earlier that the older of the two. It would seem likely that if Julien had the opportunity to take one-year-old Pierre Paschal down the Mississippi to St. Louis for baptism, he could have taken two-year-old Etienne as well.

Shortly after the 1801 baptism, Julien returned north to the Ioway territory and his trading. We know some details about his coming winter with that tribe from an account penned by British-Canadian trader Thomas G. Anderson. Born in Quèbec in 1779, upon reaching adulthood Anderson had traveled west to Mackinac Island. In late 1801 he engaged with Jacob Frank, a merchant-trader at Green Bay in the present state of Wisconsin, and was sent to winter among the Ioways on the Des Moines River. Later, Anderson wrote a narrative of his trading season.

From the Mississippi, Anderson ascended the Des Moines about fifty miles to the Ioway village located at that point. He said a "Frenchman named Julien" was his only competitor that year for the Indian trade in the area. That season the Ioways conducted their winter hunt near the Missouri River, about ninety miles across country west from their home village. Anderson explained that while being an easy enough matter, it would have been somewhat expensive to have trade goods sent around by boat up the Missouri to the vicinity of the Ioway hunting grounds. Therefore, to avoid that unnecessary expense, he and Julien made a gentleman's agreement that neither of them would send outfits there. Instead, they would both wait at the Ioway village until the coming spring, when the hunters would return and bring the furs to them.

Sometime during the ensuing winter, however, Julien and his interpreter had some sort of falling out. The result was that employee left Julien and came over to Anderson. He then proceeded to inform Anderson that he had been deceived by Julien. Julien had, in fact, earlier in the fall sent trade goods up to the Ioway hunting grounds by way of the Missouri River. Anderson was, of course, furious by this revelation, and demanded an immediate explanation from Julien. As he later wrote: "[I] showered all the abuse I could muster on his cringing head."

Led by Julien's former interpreter, Anderson and several of his men then carried on their backs seven loads of their own trade goods and tramped across country on foot to the Ioway hunting ground. Six days later, after what must have been an arduous trek through the winter cold and snow, they reached their destination and took Julien's two employees there by surprise. Not long afterward, the native hunters came in, and Anderson reported making a splendid season's trade. Julien's men, of course, continued on with their own trading, too. The competitive affair ended in at least somewhat of a spirit of cooperation. Anderson left one of his men with Julien's pair to assist in transporting both parties' accumulated packs of fur down the Missouri to St. Louis on Julien's boat.[4]

That winter's episode allows us to surmise several facts concerning Denis Julien that may be inferred, though were not specifically mentioned, in Anderson's narrative.

If Anderson's mileages are close to being accurate, the Ioway village where Julien spent the winter of 1801-02 was located on the north bank of the Des Moines River, just east of the present-day town of Ottumwa. Archeologists and historians have determined its presence there from around 1770 until 1824. Called by the Native Americans *Otawenna*, meaning simply "village," it was typical of the Ioway encampments of the time. The banks and terraces bordering the stream were used to cultivate fields of corn, beans, pumpkins, and squash. Both the men and women fished the stream and gathered shellfish, such as freshwater clams and mussels. The men also hunted both large and small game in the surrounding woodlands, from deer to rabbits and squirrels. The Ioway's dwellings were usually bowl-shaped, somewhat elongated, and built of interwoven and tied saplings. This served as a frame that was then covered over with either large slabs of cut bark or thick reed mats.

That Julien had with him an interpreter indicates two possibilities. Seemingly most obvious is that he was not as yet fluent in the Ioway language. This is somewhat hard to believe, however, considering the he had been married to an Ioway woman for several years and had probably lived much of the time with the Ioway people. What is probably the correct scenario is that his "interpreter" was actually more of a "liaison" than a true translator. Either way, this is also an indication that his wife, Catherine, and his children, were not with Julien for the winter season's trading. Otherwise she would have undoubtedly acted as both interpreter and intermediary if needed.

Perhaps most importantly, as far as Julien's career as a fur trader is concerned, is his having *engagés* actually working for him. This is the first indication that he had now expanded his "business." He was no longer working by himself as an individual, but employed others to assist him in his endeavors. Of course, if we take the narrative's assertions at face value, Julien may simply have hired the two men as needed accomplices in his scheme to deceive Anderson. In the close-knit community of the upper Mississippi fur traders, most were acquainted with and knew one another on a more-or-less personal basis. But the competition for trade with the various Native American bands and tribes made for a somewhat cutthroat business, even among "friends."

* * *

Along that portion of the Mississippi lying above St. Louis, the Des Moines River was an important locale. It provided a convenient passageway for European traders, via its western tributaries, to trails that led farther west to the Missouri River and the various tribes that inhabited what was later called the Council Bluffs area.

The French name *La Riviére des Moines* can be interpreted two ways. Literally it means "River of the Monks." However, there is no historical basis for any priests or other religious figures ever to have been established there. A more likely possibility is that the word *moines* is actually the French mistranslation of the Illini word *moingon*, meaning "mounds." Archeologists have, in fact, discovered several prehistoric, man-made earthen mounds scattered along the course of the river all the way from its mouth for over fifty miles upstream.

Because the Des Moines River was important not only as the home for several Ioway villages, but also as a significant route westward toward the Missouri, in 1799 Zenon Trudeau, the Lieutenant-Governor of Upper Louisiana, issued a grant of land near its mouth to Louis Tesson *dit* Honoré. *Dit* was one of several frustratingly confusing names usages, at least to genealogists and historians, used by the French in pre-modern times. It meant literally "called," or "known as." In this case Tesson was the actual family surname, while Honoré was simply a "nickname." In ensuing years, however, a person or family may have become known by one or even both names, depending on who was using it. Significantly, Tesson had been one of the companions of Denis Julien, who just the previous year, as reported by François Cailhol, had taken a canoe-load of furs down the Mississippi to St. Louis.

By the terms of his Spanish land grant, Tesson was required to plant trees, cultivate the soil, instruct the local Indians in agriculture, and endeavor to convert them to the Catholic faith. However, in an unwritten political directive, he was also told to keep in contact with the Ioway tribe, observe British trading operations in the Des Moines River area, and periodically report what he learned back to the Spanish authorities in St. Louis. Therefore, Tesson chose as his claim a one league square (about nine square miles) tract of land at the head of the Des Moines Rapids. This, of course, was on the west, or Spanish, side of the Mississippi, about where today's town of Montrose, Iowa, stands.

Soon after, in August of 1799, Tesson did report that another trader, Pierre Dorion, would be coming down the Illinois River to St. Louis to obtain permission to trade on the Des Moines. He warned that Dorion was actually employed by a Michilimackinac merchant, and that he planned to meet with another British trader, Lewis Crawford, who for the past several years had done his worst to prevent expansion of the French-Spanish trade with the Ioway. Interestingly, a year earlier, Dorion, too, was one of the five canoe companions of Denis Julien.

The *Rapides des Moines* was a twelve-mile-long, shallow, shoal-ridden stretch of the Mississippi stretching above the mouth of the Des Moines River. An impediment to river travel by larger keelboats and barges, especially during seasons of low water, well-beaten trails on both sides of the Mississippi were needed to connect its upriver and downriver ends. The head of the rapids was called by the Native Americans *Ahwe-pe-tuck*, "beginning of cascades," while the foot of the rapids was *Puck-a-chee-tuck*, "bottom of cascades." Also located at the head of the rapids and the beginning of the downstream trail on the west side of the Mississippi was the Sac (the English rendering of the French *Sauk*) village of *Quashqueme*, or "Jumping Fish."

At the 1794 Battle of Fallen Timbers, in present-day northwestern Ohio, the alliance of Native American tribes east of the Mississippi and north of the Ohio River, who had long been sympathetic to the British, were finally defeated by an American force under General Anthony Wayne. This victory opened the way for American settlement into what was then the Northwest Territory. Therefore, by the beginning of the 1800s, the confederated Sac-Fox tribe had been pushed westward from their historic homelands in northern Illinois and southern Wisconsin by the steadily encroaching tide of white settlers. While the main body of the tribe resided in a village near the east bank of the Mississippi in northern Illinois, the band of the Sacs under Quashqueme had now established a village on the west bank of the Mississippi. Because of this, Louis Tesson also established a trading post on his Spanish land grant, where he and his family lived for the next four years.

But there now took place a figurative political bombshell. The fuse had been quietly lit in 1800. Due to the recent takeover and subsequent grandiose ambitions of Napoléon Bonaparte, another secret treaty, this time of San Ildefonso, retroceded Louisiana from Spain and back once again to France. Spain did, however, continue to administer the territory. Then, in May of 1803, came the culminating explosion. Because of France's continued fighting in Europe and the disastrous slave rebellion in French Haiti, the Treaty of Cession sold the entire province of Louisiana to the United States. The so-called Louisiana Purchase, antedated to April 30, gave America possession of all of the lands west of the Mississippi encompassed by the drainage basin of the Missouri River. In November Spain officially transferred Louisiana back to France, and in December France, in turn, officially transferred it to the United States. However, due to the cold and harsh winter season, river traffic along the Mississippi was essentially closed down. Therefore, the earth-shaking news did not actually reach St. Louis until the early spring of 1804. The ceremonial transfers, then, from Spain to France, and thence from France to the United States, did not take place until March 9 and 10.

Not only Louisiana, but nearly the entire watershed of the Mississippi River was now in American possession. Just three months after the ceremonial territorial transfers, on June 4, 1804, Denis Julien conducted a transaction with Auguste Chouteau, now the leading fur merchant in St. Louis. He was advanced credit amounting to $56.20 for the delivery of 140 shaved deerskins.[5] This was the first time, as far as any contemporary records show, that Julien had any dealings with St. Louis businessmen. If he did so at any earlier time, when the territory was still under Spanish authority, those records are no longer extant. After the American takeover, however, such records were more assiduously kept.

The following year Julien continued on with his Ioway trading. On March 25, 1805, the new Territory of Louisiana had been created, and in April he received a trading permit from Pierre Chouteau, brother of Auguste, and now also the U.S. government's Indian Agent for the new territory. Licenses were still required of all traders, but the new United States authorities were much stricter in this regard than the previous Spanish officials had been. Julien's permit was for the area of his usual trading grounds, the "River du Moin [sic]."[6]

Noteworthy on the permit was the inclusion of a partner, Lewis Crawford. This is significant for many of Julien's future trade endeavors. Crawford was a resident of Prairie du Chien, longtime French and British trading outpost near the mouth of the Wisconsin River. More importantly, however, as far back as 1799 he was a known agent of British merchants on Mackinac Island.

In 1804 a treaty had been initiated by the new American government with the Sac-Fox tribe. It was signed on November 3 and quickly approved by the United States Congress. Terms of the treaty included agricultural and educational instruction for the natives, the payment of a small annual annuity to the tribe, and the establishment of a trading post. By 1805 the first of these provisions was implemented. William Ewing, a young Pennsylvania farmer, was hired and assigned to teach the natives both agriculture and animal husbandry. He was directed to locate on the east bank of the Mississippi River, opposite Quashqueme's Sac village, at what is now the present-day town of Nauvoo, Illinois.

Ewing arrived at the head of the Des Moines Rapids in June of 1805. He was accompanied by Louis Honoré (Tesson), who was to serve as his interpreter with the local Sac natives. It was undoubtedly Tesson *dit* Honoré's familiarity with the area that originally contributed to the decision to locate the American agricultural station at this point, almost directly across the river from what had been Tesson's home. A log house was constructed for Ewing and the facility, and though he did do a limited amount of trading with the natives, there was as yet no actual trading post.

In August, just three months after Ewing arrived at what was now simply referred to as Head of Rapids, a keelboat with a detachment of U. S. soldiers left St. Louis. Under the command of Lieutenant Zebulon M. Pike, this was a military exploratory expedition to the upper Mississippi River. On August 20 they reached the foot of the rapids and were assisted by Ewing and Tesson in negotiating their way up through the difficult, dozen-mile stretch of treacherous shoals. Pike and his men camped near Ewing's place that night, and the following day hosted a general council with all of the whites and Native American leaders of the area. It is notable that Pike did not mention or list Denis Julien as one of those in attendance at the meeting, so he very likely was not in the area at the time.

Pike's August 20 journal entry, though, does contain the significant assessment that Ewing's station would be a good position for a trading establishment. The lieutenant and his party were back in St. Louis by October. Therefore it may not be surprising that it was that same fall of 1805, that Julien did take up residence on a tract of land situated immediately below Ewing's establishment.[7] On this property, which he simply "squatted" on (it was never officially purchased), he soon erected a "one-room trading house" for him and his family.[8] This bit of oral history seems to be borne out on the 1811 map that was specially prepared and engraved for the publication of Pike's official government report. On it is clearly shown two square-shaped "building" symbols, one larger just above a smaller one. The site is labeled "U. S. Agricultural Establishment," which the larger symbol undoubtedly was. The smaller, however, matches exactly the stated location of Julien's "trading house."

Denis Julien had now embarked upon the "in between" path; what the French termed the *entre deux*. While before he had spent the vast majority of his time with the Ioways, he now would be living in the world of the white man, but, with a Native American family.

Along with the government's desire for a trading facility, Julien's decision to abandon his somewhat nomadic ways and put down more firmly set roots at the head of the Des Moines Rapids may have been prompted by his growing family. He might have recognized and seized this window of opportunity to provide a better and more settled life for his wife and children. Whatever the initial reason, Julien would live there, just above the murmuring turbulence of the rapids, for the next fourteen years.

Head of the Rapids, ca 1820s.
National Archives & Records Service
Washington, D.C.

THREE

L'ENTREPRENEUR

Except for the occasional French, British, or American trader, the west side of the Mississippi River remained nearly untouched by the hands of Europeans. Though officially a part of the Territory of Louisiana, what is today the state of Iowa was at that time still considered Indian territory. Large tracts of virgin forest remained, and oak, beech, hickory, chestnut, and elm rose up nearly a hundred feet in height. Open prairie areas farther to the west lay untouched by metal plows, and the native grasses grew as high as the proverbial "belly of a horse."

The east, Illinois side, however, was now becoming more and more settled. New trails and even rough roads branched off in all directions, and the wooded areas were splotched with the fresh clearings of incoming settlers. Julien's new location, and Ewing's, was on a bend of the Mississippi River that makes a long, smooth arc pointing toward the west and leaving a bulge of bottomland on the east side. This bottomland is shaped like a half-ellipse, some two miles long from north to south and a mile wide. A line of broken bluffs runs north and south along the east, or land side. In 1805 the low, flat area was mostly covered by brush and vegetation. A central spring was a source of water, but also made much of the land wet and marshy.

While Denis Julien would flourish in the coming years at the head of the Des Moines Rapids, William Ewing did not. Despite the good intentions of the U.S. government, stories eventually began to drift downriver to St. Louis that Ewing had become more interested in carrying on illicit trade with the natives than teaching them to farm. It was circulated that he would give them whiskey for their guns, then barter the same weapons back to them again for valuable furs. It is significant that Julien was never implicated in any such illegal trading.

Whatever the truth may have been, in 1806 Ewing was officially accused of misconduct and ultimately removed from his position by the Superintendent of Indian Affairs in St. Louis. In 1807, Nicholas Boilvin, a recently appointed Indian agent for the Sac-Fox tribe, was sent to oversee the agricultural station. The local Sac band, however, seemed to have no interest in learning horticulture, much less in adopting it as a new way of life. Finally, in the fall of 1807, the U.S. superintendent ordered the station closed.

Julien, however, stayed on with his *maison de commerce* – his trading house. The increasing scope of his activities was indicated almost immediately after his arrival at Head of Rapids. On October 21, 1805, he hired Joseph Marie as his clerk. Marie was a resident of St. Charles, Missouri, just a few miles west of St. Louis on the Missouri River. His salary was to be five hundred pounds of silver (currency), payable in pelts. Interestingly, the contract also called for Julien to give Marie and his wife "clothing appropriate for the place where they [were to] work."[1]

A type of organization, or hierarchy, had long become established since the earliest days of the fur trade in New France. In a somewhat modified form it had continued down through successive years of the industry, even into the Mississippi-Missouri River valleys. The head trader, who held a license from the government, was known as the *bourgeois*. Immediately under him were the *commis*, or clerks. They acted, as the term still means today, as keepers and recorders of the business and financial records. However, in the eighteenth and nineteenth-century fur industry, such clerks would also on occasion be sent out by the *bourgeois* as the leader of a trading expedition to a native village or hunting ground.

Thus, in 1806, Marie was dispatched by Julien to trade on the "Missouri River or its tributaries."[2] This could have been anywhere along that river, from its mouth above St. Louis to as far up its course as what Lewis and Clark, during their historic expedition to its headwaters in 1803, had called the Council Bluff in present-day eastern Nebraska. However, due to past dealings and long familiarity, certain traders usually did business with particular tribes. Therefore, Marie's destination was more than likely the Ioway hunting grounds in far western Iowa, where Julien's two *engagés* had traded in the contentious winter of 1801-02.

1807 was a busy and no doubt tumultuous year for Julien. On May 1, another daughter, named Marguerite, was born to Denis and Catherine.[3]

By the end of the month, on the 26th, it is shown that Julien was in St. Louis and was paid $23 by Pierre Chouteau. This entry appears in the ledger book of Chouteau's fur company and is included in a list of payments. Unfortunately, however, it does not show what the payment was for.[4] Due to the spring date, it may have been for at least a small portion of the furs gathered by Julien the previous season.

Sometime during the next four weeks, Julien traveled northward several hundred miles to Mackinac Island. By the early 1800s this shortened form of the name Michilimackinac was customarily used in ordinary conversation. Though he almost had to have been in Michilimackinac sometime early in his life and fur trade career, the first actual contemporary record of Julien's being there appears in the notary book of Samuel Abbott. Entries therein show that from June 26 through August 1, he hired twelve *engagés* to work for him at various locales during the upcoming fur season.[5]

According to a legal system which had been in place since French times, both British, and now American authorities required that, before embarking on ventures into the interior, the new employees sign before a notary public a formal contract with their employer. The details of this agreement were then entered into the official notebook of the notary. These contracts, or "engagements," were the source of the French fur trade term *engagé*. The employees hired by Julien and other traders were not local Mackinac men, but probably came from Montréal and Québec.

One of the entries in the Mackinac notary book was the destination, or wintering ground, of the new *engagé*. It is indicative of the growing scope of Julien's trading business to note the places to be visited by the twelve men hired by him in 1807. Seven were bound for the Mississippi, one for the Missouri, and one for the Wisconsin River. These are all known trading areas. The wintering ground for the last three *engagés*, however, all hired on August 1, was shown as "Miss. Vellisou."[6] This is a now unknown geographical name.

"Miss." could be an abbreviation for the Missouri River. "Vellisou" is perhaps the French rendering of the Spanish surname Villasur. In 1720, near present-day Columbus, Nebraska, on the Platte River about 70 miles west of the Missouri, Lieutenant-General Pedro de Villasur and a military expedition from Santa Fe were defeated by a French force and their Indian allies. Perhaps, then, in 1807 the name "Vellisou" referred to a particular geographic region bordering the Missouri River on the west, not far from the traditional western hunting grounds of the Ioway tribe.

Julien's presence in Mackinac from July 26 until August 1 does explain a seeming incongruity in the baptismal record of his daughter Marguerite. According to the archives of the St. Louis Church, Marguerite was baptized on July 28, and therefore her father, obviously, could not have been in attendance. This, then, is undoubtedly why Julien's signature does not appear at the bottom of the baptismal record, as it had in the entries of his first three children.

Julien's license to trade for the upcoming 1807-08 season was obtained from the U.S. Superintendent of Indian Affairs in St. Louis on September 22. The tribes he was to be allowed to trade with are listed as the Sioux and Ioways.[7] This confirms the wintering grounds listed in Samuel Abbott's Mackinac notary book. The Ioways, as already seen, ranged from the Mississippi on the east to the Missouri River to the west. The larger Sioux tribe was made up of seven separate bands, roughly divided into three different divisions depending upon their location. Julien and his men, therefore, would have been dealing with the Santee Sioux division, which at that time was located in what is now southern Minnesota, southwestern Wisconsin, and northern Iowa.

The late summer of 1808 found Julien again far to the north at Mackinac. There, once more, he hired workers for the coming trading season. On August 15 and 16 he engaged nine men to winter on the Mississippi.[8]

Though he had probably done so in 1807 also, this year while at the Great Lakes trading center, Julien purchased items of merchandise to take back south with him. One such memorandum, or invoice, serves as a good example of just what sort of goods were involved in Julien's trade: Three 2½-point blankets; six ells of woolen cloth; four yards of plaid linen; two yards of green flannel; one half-dozen buttons; one [roll] of sewing thread; the "makings" for three capotes; the "makings" for three pantaloons; three yards of ribbon, fifteen [wheels? blocks?] of cheese; 28 yards of calico; three [tubes? jars?] of vermilion; two dozen knives; 100 needles; 150 pounds of sugar; two [reams? boxes?] of writing paper; sixty-six gallons of whiskey; and six gallons of double-distilled spirits.[9]

For the past two years, and for the next three to come, Mackinac was to be one constant in the fur-trading life of Denis Julien.

* * *

This narrow, keystone point between three of the Great Lakes and the watersheds of the St. Lawrence and upper Mississippi Rivers, has had a long and tumultuous history. The first trading house that had been established at Michilimackinac by La Salle in 1679 was used for several years. Its location was on the mainland, just south of actual Mackinac Island. The post was reestablished in 1713 as a French fort, also known as Michilimackinac. In 1763, however, the end of the French and Indian War placed it into British hands. In 1780, during the American war for independence, the decision was made to abandon the vulnerable wooden fort on the mainland and build a new stone-block fortification out on Mackinac Island.

The new site was just inland from a good landing place in a small cove on the southeast shore of the six square-mile island. Ships and boats would be somewhat protected from the weather by a small, rounded island just a few hundred yards distant, and steep limestone cliffs sheltered both sides of the cove. In between lay a smooth beach and a strip of open meadowland where Native Americans often camped. Behind these flats rose a steep hill some 150 feet high. Where this slope leveled off just short of the actual summit was the site chosen for the new fort.

The fur business of Michilimackinac simply followed the military out onto Mackinac Island. A new village of small homes and larger warehouses quickly took shape along the bend of the cove. The habitations by no means filled the entire area, and there was room at either end for visiting natives to set up temporary encampments. Mackinac was, and continued to be, the great place of arrival and departure for the upper Mississippi fur trade. From here the traders set out for their destinations, and here, after a year's absence, they returned with their pelts.

The 1783 Treaty of Paris granted the victorious new American nation all territory south of the Great Lakes. However, because of imprecise mapping and unclear language in the treaty, the British remained in control of the region even after the American Revolution. They also refused to evacuate their various forts, including Mackinac. The English government's stated reason was that it was keeping the posts as security for debts allegedly owed by the United States to deposed Loyalists. Therefore, the St. Louis traders once again began dealing with British merchants at Mackinac.

Eventually, however, overburdened by the Napoleonic wars in Europe and because of the decisive 1794 American defeat of the British-supported Indian tribes in what was then the American northwest, the British government decided to no longer press the issue. Just three months later American diplomat John Jay concluded with Great Britain what came to be known as the Jay Treaty. In it reciprocal trading rights were established, and traders from either nation were to be allowed to enter the territory of the other to engage with the native tribes. Finally, it was also agreed that all British forts in American territory would be evacuated by 1796. The United States officially took over control of Mackinac, then, in October of that year.

For most of any given year, while the *voyageurs* and traders were scattered to their various trading grounds, the population of Mackinac was relatively sparse. However, during the weeks of *rendezvous*, as there had been in July and August for decades, there might be almost a thousand fur men and an equal number of natives in and about the town, where they traded, feasted, drank, gambled, and caroused until exhaustion. This was their great annual *rêverie*, their *régal*, after a long winter and spring of back-breaking and freezing work. Business-wise, the traders came to deposit their accumulated furs at the warehouses and then secure new outfits of goods and merchandise for the coming season.

Here, too, the traders would hire new *engagés*, who historically signed on for only a year at a time. These employees typically tended to shift from one employer to another, rarely staying more than a single season with the same *bourgeois*. This was the time each year, then, when Julien would journey north to Mackinac to secure men for his trading season. While it would have seemed more convenient, and closer, to hire workers in the St. Louis area, Julien evidently chose not to do so. Perhaps he enjoyed the annual festive get-togethers at Mackinac, and just maybe it was due to remembered ancestral ties to French Canada in his past.

* * *

While Julien's nine new *engagés* conducted the season's trading, Julien himself seems to have begun, in modern-day business terminology, to diversify. During the winter of 1808-09 he was contracted to provide sleds and oxen to assist in the erection of the palisades for a new United States fort on the Mississippi River. The military facility was actually being built as a secondary consideration in the implementation of the United States factory trading system.

First conceived of by President George Washington in 1795, such a system, he theorized, would furnish Native Americans with merchandise at cost and, perhaps more importantly, protect them from the nefarious influence of unscrupulous traders. He hoped that by dealing fairly with the natives to win over their friendship to the fledgling United States from the previous British regime. But it was not until 1802 that President Thomas Jefferson convinced Congress to pass a bill to actually implement the scheme. That year the first four such factories were built in the South. The term factory is somewhat misleading, as they were simply large trading posts. No goods or merchandise were actually manufactured at these facilities. In 1803, following the Louisiana Purchase, a new congressional act was passed authorizing the establishment of more such factories.

In 1808 it was decided to erect a government trading factory on the Mississippi River somewhere in the vicinity of the Des Moines Rapids. This would allow American traders to enter the region and compete with the British, who by terms of the Jay Treaty were still allowed to operate inside of U.S. boundaries. In addition, a military post was also to be built for the protection of the trading establishment.

On September 26, a military contingent under the command of First Lieutenant Alpha Kingsley arrived at the site selected for the factory and fort, on the west side of the Mississippi River some ten miles upstream from the head of the Des Moines Rapids. He called it Belle Vue, soon contracted to just Bellevue, and work began almost immediately. This included the preparation of white oak logs, from twelve to eighteen inches in diameter, cut to a uniform length of fourteen feet, hewed flat on both sides, and stripped of their bark. It was not easy to find trees that met these specifications for the palisade timbers, and many were felled some distance from the actual building site. That winter of 1808-09 was one of the worst that the upper Mississippi valley had seen in many years. Snow fell early and deep, and the military work parties soon found it nearly impossible to transport the large logs. Thus the hiring of Julien in the early spring to supply sleds and oxen to get the large logs moved in so that actual construction could take place.[10]

The fortification was completed by April of 1809 and officially named Fort Madison, after the new President of the United States. With the protective military installation in place, work could now begin on the trading factory itself. It was determined that the building would be located outside of the fort's walls, so that visiting natives would have less access to the interior defenses. The trade warehouse, however, was put inside. Work, though, progressed slowly, and even the soldiers themselves were sometimes recruited to help in the construction when they were off duty. Finally, Denis Julien was once again hired, this time to provide civilian laborers on the trading factory and houses.[11]

The harsh winter may also have had a tragic effect in the personal life of Julien and his family. On February 13, 1809, a brief entry in the burial records of the St. Louis Church records the death of Paschal Julien, the young eight-year-old son of Denis and Catherine.[12] No cause of death is given, but the brutal winter perhaps played some contributing factor.

Though the trading factory itself would not be completed for several more months, the civilian factor, John W. Johnson, was already doing business with the surrounding native tribes. Soon, Denis Julien was hired to freight fifty-one packs of "peltries and furs" for Johnson from Fort Madison down the Mississippi River to St. Louis.[13] While the numbers involved are much higher, it is informative to see just what types of accumulated furs were being shipped by Johnson. They would be reflective of what Julien, though on a smaller scale, would have been dealing with in his personal trading business.

A March 28, 1809 report from Johnson lists 710 pounds of beaver; 1,353 muskrat skins; 3,585 raccoon skins; 25,021 pounds of shaved deerskins; 3,000 pounds of deerskins with hair; 64 bear skins; 176 other skins; 100 pounds of beeswax; and 968 pounds of tallow. The beaver, of course, would be mainly for high-grade, more expensive hats; the muskrat skins for lower-grade, more common everyday hats; the raccoon skins for rough headgear and heavy gloves; the many deerskins for tanned leather clothes and lighter gloves; and the bear skins for rugs and heavy coats.

The last part of July and the first week in August found Julien once again up north at Mackinac, where he hired men for the upcoming trading season on the Mississippi.[14] Though he was about three months too early, November of 1809 saw the opening of the U.S. government's latest trading factory, this time at Mackinac. And Julien himself was also expanding his own trading business. He now maintained "houses" just outside of the walls at Fort Madison.[15] It is not known whether these were for his hired workers on the trading factory building, or possibly facilities for his own private trading interests. It may very well have been a combination of both.

1810 was much the same for Julien as the previous year. He continued to maintain houses at Fort Madison,[16] and he still traveled up to Mackinac in the late summer to hire men for the trading season on the Mississippi.[17] His license for that year, issued in St. Louis on October 14, was for his regular customers, the Ioways and Sioux.[18]

In March of 1811, Julien was again hired by John Johnson, the Fort Madison factor, to freight some furs downriver to St. Louis. On this occasion it was seven packs of raccoon skins.[19] While Julien made his usual trip upriver to Mackinac in August, later that fall found him engaged in yet another enterprise that shows his increasing business diversity. In November he shipped, not furs, but lead ingots down to St. Louis.[20]

By 1811 the northern band of the Sac-Fox tribe were turning more and more to the mining of lead to use in trade for manufactured goods. It was even noted by the U.S. Indian agent that they were, therefore, doing less and less hunting and trapping for furs. Extensive bodies of lead ore had been discovered in the vicinity of present-day Dubuque, Iowa, on the west side of the Mississippi, and today's Galena, Illinois, on the east bank. Only a thin overburden of dirt covered these deposits. The local natives would scrape this soil off with bone hoes, chip the crumbly ore into baskets, and drag them on sledges to their encampments. There they would throw the chunks of ore into large fires. When the resulting embers finally cooled, the solidified lumps of lead that had melted free from the surrounding rock were carefully picked out. Formed into crude bars, the lead could now be exchanged with white traders.

The 358 bars of lead shipped by Julien in the fall of 1811 had been ordered by William Clark back in February. Clark, of Lewis and Clark expedition fame, was now not only U.S. Superintendent of Indian Affairs in St. Louis, but also the St. Louis agent of the Missouri Fur Company. His order for a supply of lead, then, could simply have been for a salable commodity for this private business. At this time that metal was in high demand for the making of lead shot and bullets, for both the regular military and the territorial militia.

Events of the coming year would bear this out.

Michilimackinac, 1820s.
Meade C. Williams, *Early Mackinac*
St. Louis, Mo.: Buschart Bros, & Co., 1903.

FOUR:

AMI OU ENNEMI

On June 12, 1812, United States President James Madison signed a proclamation of war against Great Britain. The conflict came to an end some two-and-a-half years later, though it has come to be known as the War of 1812.

This was no sudden boiling-over between the two countries. Bad feelings had simmered since the 1783 end of the Revolutionary War. Certain elements of the British government had never completely accepted the American colonies' independence and looked on the affair as not really an English military loss, but merely a political concession. Ongoing reasons for the 1812 hostilities were predominantly three-fold: English impressments of naturalized Americans of British origin; the United States' desire to claim more land for settlement; and an end to Britain's continued support of Native American opposition to the new country's westward expansion.

American traders, especially in the upper Mississippi region, were caught in the middle. This was especially true of those, such as Denis Julien, who had business ties with both St. Louis and Mackinac. Also caught-up in this tug-of-allegiance was the Ioway tribe, which resided in American territory, but maintained historic ties to British trading interests. Ever since the Jay Treaty of 1794, which allowed English traders to continue to operate inside of American territory, they also continued to foment and stir-up dissatisfaction and unrest among all of the upper Mississippi tribes.

Therefore, as far back as 1808 the new Louisiana Territorial Governor, Meriwether Lewis, of Lewis and Clark expedition fame, conceived the plan of using both American and former English traders to exert their influence to try and sway the Ioways toward the United States. One of these intermediaries was Denis Julien. In an August, 1808, letter to Secretary of War Henry Dearborn in Washington, D.C., Lewis stated: "I employed also the friendly aid of Mr. Julian [sic], an old and much respected trader among the Ioways...."[1] The use of the term "old" in this case probably did not refer to Julien's age, which would have been approximately 35 in 1808, but most likely was reflective of his long association with the Ioway tribe.

Due to both British propaganda spread by its traders and the continued expansion of American settlement, hostile incidents between whites and Native Americans were inevitable. Following his arrival as governor early in 1808, Meriwether Lewis had been compelled to call out the territorial militia three times just that first year. In March, 1809, hostile activity of a band of Winnebago to the northeast of Fort Madison was brought to the attention of its commander, Lieutenant Kingsley. Thoroughly alarmed, he sent an urgent dispatch downriver to Governor Lewis and Indian Superintendent Clark alerting them of a possible attack.

The message arrived in St. Louis about the first of April, and on April 3, Lewis called for the immediate raising of two volunteer companies, from both that town and nearby St. Charles, to help protect the frontier. An April 19 list of volunteers in St. Louis contains nineteen names, at the head of which is "Dennis Jullien [sic]."[2] This particular company was for "light infantry," whose duty was to provide an advance screen ahead of the main body of troops, harassing and delaying an opposing force.

Governor Lewis alerted all volunteer companies of cavalry, riflemen, and infantry in the territory to be ready to march at a moment's notice. On April 21 he issued a general order for the muster of all companies on May 4. By the middle of May, however, tensions had eased somewhat, and subsequent reinforcements for Fort Madison were of regular Army soldiers, not volunteer companies. Therefore, a letter carried by Denis Julien in early October of 1809, from Acting Governor Frederick Bates to the new commander at Fort Madison, Captain Horatio Stark, was evidently merely an act of convenience rather than military duty. Denis Julien was entrusted with the delivery of this letter as he was soon to be leaving St. Louis on his way upriver to the Des Moines Rapids area.[3]

* * *

In 1811, Nicholas Boilvin, now the U. S. Indian Agent at Prairie du Chien, reported that each year the various Indian tribes met in council there to discuss and settle their affairs and to decide on future courses of action. That summer the story had been spread that soon the "English father" would declare war against the Americans and once again would take the Mississippi tribes under his protection. If they sided with the English they would have everything in abundance. Complaints had been raised that the Americans had blocked all of the rivers, so that only a few English traders could reach the tribes. The majority of the natives still preferred the better-made British merchandise to American-produced trade goods, which were of an inferior quality.

The first openly voiced accusation of Denis Julien being allied with the British was heard soon after Boilvin's report. An anonymous writer, who simply signed himself "A Democrat," penned a disgruntled epistle to now Secretary of War John Armstrong in early October of 1811. In it the person detailed many complaints about the conditions at Fort Madison and against its commanding officer, Captain Stark, as well as a serious allegation concerning Denis Julien. The writer maintained that a "Monsr. Julien, a Frenchman & British trader," was soon to be recommended as the civilian sutler to the military at the fort.[4] Perhaps this unknown person remembered Julien's partnership, back in 1805, with Lewis Crawford, who *was* a British trader. As events transpired, Julien was not appointed to the sutler's position, and very probably was never even considered for it. But rumors and stories of his being a British sympathizer would continue to follow him for the next several years.

A single sentence contained in a brief article of a St. Louis newspaper on September 19, 1812, was the precursor to a much more serious charge. It said merely that the previous Sunday, September 13, a barge from Mackinac, laden with maple sugar and other goods, had been seized in St. Louis. What was not stated was to whom the barge belonged – Denis Julien.

On September 30, Julien was formally indicted by the St. Louis court for "Offense against Non-intercourse Act." This act had been passed by Congress in 1809 as a trade embargo against Great Britain. In Julien's present case, it was alleged that he had transported merchandise from British-controlled Mackinac into United States territory in violation of this act. Because of the declaration of war, anti-British public sentiment was very much against any possible trafficking with English traders. Local lawyer Rufus Easton even refused to act as attorney for Julien when he was asked to do so.[5]

It was a classic case of being in the wrong place at the wrong time. In witness testimonies given at a deposition hearing before Judge John C. B. Lucas in St. Louis, the complete story was finally brought out.[6]

Julien had departed St. Louis sometime during the last part of June, 1812, on his way up to Mackinac. Word of the United States' declaration of war against Great Britain did not arrive in the Mississippi River town until July 9. On his way upriver, on July 10 Julien left "goods" at his houses at Fort Madison. Included were 100 pounds of flour and 100 pounds of salt "for the Indians."[7] Significantly, he then did not arrive at Mackinac until July 19, two days *after* the American fort there had been captured by British troops on the 17th. He was allowed, however, to proceed on with his purchasing and acquired several barrels of Indian, or maple sugar, from the U.S. trading factory on the island. Also taken on were close to a dozen "riggings" and boxes of other goods and merchandise, all together worth about $1,000. Some of this cargo was Julien's and some he was transporting for other St. Louis traders.

Julien left Mackinac somewhere between August 15 and the 20th, which was the normal departure time for all of the traders following the annual *rendezvous*, be they American or British. He returned the usual way, following the western shore of Lake Michigan and ascending Green Bay and the Fox River to *Le Portage*. There his boat and loads were seen being carried across the mile-and-a-quarter overland crossing to the Wisconsin River drainage. At the mouth of that river he again was seen making a short detour north, evidently to the town of Prairie du Chien, just a short distance up the Mississippi. Then it was once more back down that river to his next stop at Fort Madison. Unlike at Mackinac, however, here Julien found that he had, in this instance, fortuitously been at the right place at the right time.

On September 5, while Julien was still making his way downriver from Prairie du Chien, Fort Madison had been attacked by bands of the Winnebago and Fox tribes. One soldier, who was outside of the garrison at the time, was killed, and a constant firing on both sides was kept up until dark. The next morning the attack commenced again, and the Indians set fire to several boats which were tied up along the bank of the river. They also "plundered and burnt Mr. Julian's [sic] houses." The following day more of the buildings that stood outside of the garrison's walls were set on fire, but the fort itself was kept safe. The fourth day only occasional shooting was heard from the Indians, and a number were seen crossing back over the river to the east side. Finally, by September 9, the attack on the fort ended.[8]

Just a few days later, then, Julien arrived at Fort Madison on his journey downriver. While no doubt dismayed to find that his houses there had been burned, he must have been equally as relieved to learn that the goods he had left on his trip upstream were safe. They had been taken inside the walls to the factory warehouse in late August, when the first news of a possible attack had reached the fort. Retrieving the packs from the trade warehouse, Julien soon continued on down to St. Louis and the subsequent confiscation of his boat and cargo.

From the depositions and testimonies given before Judge Lucas, it soon became apparent that upon leaving St. Louis in late June, Mackinac was still in American hands and under American control. When Julien arrived there on July 19, he had no way of knowing of the British capture just two days earlier. And when he transported goods back down to St. Louis, he was at all times within American boundaries. Therefore, it was rather obvious that there, in fact, had been no violation of the Non-intercourse Act. Judge Lucas subsequently dismissed the charge and Julien did not have to face trial.

There is an informative footnote to this case involving Denis Julien. When he had approached attorney Rufus Easton to possibly represent him, he was accompanied by Patrick Lee, a St. Louis merchant and broker who was also heavily involved in the fur trade. Tellingly, Lee was there to act as an "interpreter." Evidently, even after some eight years of American rule, Julien was still not confident enough with his English to trust himself entirely to make arrangements for a lawyer.[9]

* * *

1813 was a time of comings and goings in the upper Mississippi valley. In July and August bands of the Sac-Fox tribe had made their way south and fought skirmishes with U.S. troops and settlers as far as the Missouri River. All summer U.S. Indian Agent Nicholas Boilvin and Fort Madison factor John W. Johnson worked diligently to pry the various bands of the Sac-Fox away from British influence. They were eventually successful, at least partly so. In late September a large band of Sac, as well as a smaller group of the Fox, migrated down the Mississippi and eventually settled on the south bank of the Missouri River in what is now Moniteau County.

Feelings within the Ioway tribe were also divided. French-American traders, acting as informants for the United States, reported that those natives were split, part for peace with the Americans, part for war. It is probable that the two main Ioway villages, one on the Des Moines River (visited by Julien in 1801-02) and one on the Iowa River farther north, represented these opposing points of view. The latter was probably pro-British because of its ready accessibility to Prairie du Chien and the British traders located there.

In the summer of 1813, William Clark, now governor of the new Territory of Missouri, persuaded the pro-American part of the Ioway tribe to leave the Des Moines River area and move westward to their longtime hunting grounds on the Missouri River. This in part was to distance them from the pro-British band on the Iowa River. Some of these Ioways, however, instead moved southwest to the Grand River in northwestern Missouri.

In the midst of all of these shifts of various Native American tribal bands, there was a sighting of Denis Julien. On August 20, he was in St. Louis, where he testified as a witness in a land case.[10] He had no doubt been called because of his longtime familiarity with the middle Mississippi River area even back to Spanish ownership of the region.

At this point in the war military engagements between American and British forces had taken place predominantly back east, while naval clashes between the two countries occurred along the Atlantic coast and on the Great Lakes. Fighting in the Mississippi valley, however, was mostly in the form of British-inspired Indian raids coming down from the north.

Here, in September of 1813, occurred the greatest loss so far by actual American troops. As they had the year before, a large force of Winnebago, Fox, and some Sac, once again besieged Fort Madison. This time the decision was ultimately made to abandon the post. To keep the installation from falling into British hands, under cover of darkness it was set afire and burned by the retreating American troops. One stone chimney remained standing for many years afterward, and to the traders who passed up and down the Mississippi, the site became known as Lone Chimney. To the Sac-Fox natives, however, it was called *Po-to-wo-cock*, meaning the "place of fire."

As the war between the United States and Great Britain entered its third year, 1814 saw more actual military activity in the upper Mississippi valley than ever before. In May and June, William Clark led an American force up the river and succeeded in capturing the British fort at Prairie du Chien. The very next month, however, much to the chagrin of the American populace in St. Louis, British troops easily retook the fortification.

After three years of warfare, a peace treaty was finally signed by the two nations on December 24, 1814. British forces had achieved military success in the upper Mississippi valley, while the American navy prevailed in most of the naval engagements. In the Atlantic coast area, both sides saw triumphs and defeats. Therefore, the Treaty of Ghent provided for the principle of *status quo antebellum* – the restoration of prewar territorial positions and conditions. Article 1 of the treaty specifically required that all territory and possessions taken by either country from the other during the war be restored immediately. The United States, then, did not gain new settlement areas in Canada, but, perhaps more importantly, native opposition to American expansion into the Ohio River valley was largely stopped.

When Denis Julien departed sometime in the late fall of 1814 on that season's trading expedition, the treaty ending the war had not yet been signed. As the winter of 1814-15 wore on, there was no way he could have heard about it, deep as he was, once again, in Indian territory. Indeed, news of the treaty signing did not even reach the Atlantic seaboard of the United States until February of 1815, and did not make its way to the upper Mississippi River valley area until later that spring.

The war had greatly affected the fur trade of the region, and when Julien, his son Etienne, and three or four other *engagés* ascended the Missouri River to the new villages of the Ioway tribe, they were poorly supplied with merchandise. They reportedly told the natives that the Americans had few goods with which to supply them, and that only their "English father" had plenty of trade goods. The following spring Julien and his party purchased horses from the Ioways, intent upon traveling eastward to Prairie du Chien. They never arrived, and it was widely believed that they had been intercepted on the way by a party of Indians sent by "the Americans."[11]

This information concerning Julien's 1814-15 winter trading season was contained in a letter from Duncan Graham, a British trader at Prairie du Chien, to his superiors at Mackinac. It is the only unbiased, contemporary account of possible British leanings by Julien before or during the War of 1812. And even his reported words were not so much traitorous as a truthful telling of the actual facts. During the war years American fur-merchants in St. Louis were poorly supplied with trade merchandise, while the British traders at Prairie du Chien and Mackinac were much better off. Julien had long been associated with the Ioway tribe and, of course, even had marital ties with them. He may very likely, then, have simply been trying to look after their best interests.

So, was Denis Julien a "friend or enemy" of the United States? There is, of course, no clear-cut, yes or no answer to this question. Circumstantial evidence may point to the latter, primarily from his many dealings with British traders at Mackinac. But that was purely a business decision, not a political statement. His own actions, from his being entrusted to help sway the allegiance of the Ioway tribe to the United States, to his assistance in the construction of a U.S. military fort, would seem to indicate a sincere willingness to work for and with American interests. And if he was an English sympathizer, the burning of his buildings at Fort Madison by British-backed Indians, was certainly an unusual way of rewarding him.

Denis Julien was most likely doing what the French in North America, and especially the Mississippi valley region, had been doing for most of the preceding century. They had proven to be remarkably adaptable to governmental and political changes, whether under the original French, later British, then Spanish, and finally American regimes. Julien was probably simply biding his time and weighing his options, waiting to see what the ultimate outcome of the affair was to be. Would the fortunes of war favor *les Anglais* or *les Américains*?

* * *

Whatever Julien may have thought about the overall grand scheme of world events, more mundane, but closer to home, matters also concerned him. In a March, 1815, issue of a St. Louis newspaper, he placed a notice about a lost watch. It was said to have been lost the last part of February between the River des Peres and the town of St. Charles and was described as being a "valuable silver-covered watch." A reward of $20 for its return was offered.[12]

This may be somewhat significant in two ways. A valuable, silver-covered watch might not have been the type of timepiece usually carried by a relatively humble fur trader such as Julien. Perhaps, then, it was an heirloom passed down through his family. The sum of the reward offered is also somewhat surprising. Twenty dollars in 1815 was the equivalent of over three hundred dollars in today's financial market. This would have been a rather large sum in Julien's time and, again, may have been indicative of sentimental value and not just actual monetary worth.

While the Treaty of Ghent in December, 1814 officially brought what was sometimes called the Second War of Independence to a close, as far as the upper Mississippi valley was concerned the conflict had definitely not ended. The hostile native tribes of the region had experienced no crushing military defeat, and many were still very much in rebellion against any American control. But the treaty also prohibited any actions by the United States military, territorial or federal, pending future treaties with the former native allies of the English. In fact, the boldest attacks of the entire war period in what was now Missouri Territory occurred during the six months of 1815 that intervened between the signing of the treaty and the beginning of peace negotiations with the various upper Mississippi valley tribes.

One such raid took place in early April at Côte sans Dessein, a small village and trading depot on the north bank of the Missouri River some 125 miles west of St. Louis. A contingent of Missouri "Rangers," a special unit of the territorial militia, quickly came to their aid. While scouting and camping in the area during the days following the attack, the ranger unit was delivered supplies by Denis Julien.[13]

Peace talks with the upper Mississippi tribes finally began in mid-summer of 1815. The area at Portage des Sioux, a narrow strip of low land separating the Missouri and Mississippi Rivers a few miles north of St. Louis, was chosen as the site for the peace sessions. A dozen or more tribes were represented during the opening round of talks which convened on July 10. Those tribes who did not attend were given a thirty-day notice to appear, and a second round of negotiations with an additional half-dozen or so bands commenced at the end of August. The treaty with the Ioway tribe was signed on September 16. Of the twelve individuals who were invited to serve as witnesses to the signing, one was Denis Julien.[14] His long association with the Ioways was no doubt the reason for his inclusion.

For the next two or three years, Julien continued to trade almost exclusively with the Ioway tribe. The band of the pro-American Sacs and Foxes that had moved south in 1813 were also included in his trading realm. However, even though he continued to stay on at his residence/trading depot at the head of the Des Moines Rapids, Julien now shifted his actual area of trading away from the Mississippi and its tributaries west to those of the Missouri. The Ioways now had villages in the Council Bluffs area on the Missouri itself and also on the Grand and Chariton Rivers near where those streams empty into the Missouri from the north. The smaller Sac-Fox group also had encampments on the Chariton.

About the first of June, 1816, Julien and his "crew" of traders were seen at Boone's Lick, just north of the Missouri River along Salt Creek. They were reported to have come from the Grand River, where they had no doubt been trading with the Ioways.[15] That fall, on September 6, Julien was issued a license for "Indian trade" with the "Sacs, Foxes & Ayouas [sic]" on the "Missouri."[16] Just three days later, no doubt while he was still in St. Louis, Julien sold "three deer skins... red in the hair" to Charles Gratiot for $2.50 apiece.[17]

Charles Gratiot was originally a merchant of Kaskaskia and Cahokia in the Illinois country during the 1770s. In 1781 he married a daughter of Pierre Lacléde and Marie Chouteau, and the following year the couple moved across the Mississippi to St. Louis. There Gratiot eventually became one of the leading fur merchants of that town. In 1816, the firm of Berthold & Chouteau contracted with fur baron John Jacob Astor's American Fur Company in New York City to be their importing agent for trade goods and commission seller of furs. As a result, Gratiot was made Astor's western representative in St. Louis.

Julien's sale to Gratiot of just three deerskins was, obviously, a very minor transaction. It may be looked upon, and probably was, what might be termed a "special order." The so-called *peaux rouge*, "red skins," were actually the tinge of that color assumed by the normal, out-of-season summer deer. With their slight coloration, these deerskins could be made into specialty leather items such as more upscale gloves and shoes. Though still secondary to beaver pelts, of course, the vast number of deer in the Mississippi valley region did make for a significant and profitable trade in deerskins for various leather goods.

In October of 1817, Julien received his now annual license to trade with the Native Americans. Once more it was for "the Indians on waters of [the] Missouri."[18] Though it was not specifically stated, this again would have been principally with the Ioway tribe. If any lingering rumors were still adrift about Julien's possible past sympathies for the British, they certainly in no way hindered his continuing trade business.

Fort Madison, 1810.
Courtesy of State Historical Society of Iowa
Des Moines, Iowa.

FIVE

LE LITIGATEUR

The fourteen years that Denis Julien lived at the head of the Des Moines Rapids on the Mississippi must have been among the happiest and most contented of his life. He was with his wife and children; they lived in a permanent home; and his trading business continued to prosper. It was this latter, however, in his role of a *commerçant*, or businessman, that did provide Julien with some headaches. Then, as now, the growth of a business, the hiring of employees, and especially the contracting with other individuals for work to be done, inevitably led to litigation in court. Between 1805 and 1819, Julien was involved in no less than nine such judicial cases. While at first seemingly minor events in his overall career, the depositions and transcripts from these lawsuits do provide some personal glimpses into not only Julien's life, but also the inner workings of the fur trade itself.

The first litigation that there is record of is a June 23, 1808, suit filed by Julien against Bazil [sic] Hebert for $275. Hebert was a member of a French-Canadian family which had come to St. Louis by the early 1790s and where they engaged in the fur trade. The 1808 suit actually had its beginnings some two years earlier. In August and October of 1806, before the upcoming winter trading season, Hebert had signed three promissory notes to Julien for delivery of a certain amount and kind of furs the next spring. This type of contract was typical of the fur business, whether it involved large companies such as the Chouteaus and Robidouxs in St. Louis and David Stone in Mackinac, or the smaller merchants such as Denis Julien. They would provide trade goods to individuals or small groups of traders on credit, and in return would receive a certain percentage of the upcoming season's fur take.

It is informative to see what kinds of furs were involved in the three contracts: Nine bear skins of the value of $36; seventy red deerskins worth $20; and seventy-eight pounds of beaver furs worth $156. It is also interesting to note that these "dollars" were to be in "currency of the United States," as opposed to French dollars, *livres*, sometimes referred to in French-Canadian idiom as *piastres*. According to Julien's suit, repeated requests for either the sums of money or the skins and furs had been ignored.[1]

On May 13, 1809, Julien filed another suit against Hebert, this time along with Joseph Papin and Jean Baptiste Lacroix as co-defendants, for $250. In June of the previous year, after Julien had filed his first suit, Hebert had approached the two men to cover his debt to Julien for at least one of his 1806 notes. Papin was the son of well-known St. Louis fur trader Joseph Marie Papin, while Lacroix was a veteran fur trader who had been in St. Louis as early as 1770. The three had signed a promissory note to deliver to Julien seventy-eight pounds of beaver fur, or to pay its monetary value, by March 1, 1809. This would have been, of course, the spring following the 1808-09 winter trading season. Once again, however, the date for fulfillment of the new promissory note had passed, and repeated requests to the three individuals had been unanswered.

Hebert was subsequently taken into custody by the district sheriff, and writs were also issued for Papin and Lacroix. Though it is not detailed in the official records, some sort of out-of-court settlement must have been reached. On May 22, a written request from Julien and his attorney was sent to the sheriff, asking for Hebert's release and cancellation of the writs against Papin and Lacroix.[2]

On July 26, however, Hebert turned around and filed suit against Julien. Even though the original debts had seemingly been satisfied, Hebert evidently felt he had suffered unnecessary duress from his arrest and incarceration, if only for a brief time. His suit was in the amount of $15.95 for "costs in a certain suit expend," and a writ was issued for Julien. As of August 2, though, the district sheriff, William Sherry, reported that the writ had not been served.

Hebert, therefore, refiled his suit on January 15, 1810, this time for the amount of $18.05. But once again, by January 26 the sheriff reported that the writ could not be served. As he put it in official legal terms, "Neither body nor property found." The reasons for these two failures are easy enough to explain. In July and August of 1809, Julien was far to the north at Mackinac, hiring *engagés* for his trading business. In January of 1810, he was also upriver, this time at Fort Madison. The St. Charles district sheriff did not have the authority to serve the writ if the receiver was outside of his jurisdiction.

However, Hebert was persistent, if nothing else. He filed suit yet again on April 11 for the growing amount of $20.05. This time Julien was evidently in the St. Louis area, and the writ was successfully executed by the sheriff.[3] No other records of the case are given, and there was evidently no trial or verdict rendered. This would seem to indicate that, once more, the claim was very likely settled out-of-court.

It was some three years later that Julien again filed suit against a presumed debtor. This was on August 26, 1813, against Auguste Chouteau and Julien Dubuque "deceased." Dubuque had died on March 24, 1810, and, having left no will, Auguste Chouteau had been appointed administrator of his estate.

Julien Dubuque was born in Québec in 1762 and had come south to the upper Mississippi region by 1788. In that year he was given permission by the local Fox band to mine the valuable lead ore to be found within their territory in present-day northeast Iowa. He settled at what is now the town of Dubuque on the Mississippi River, and eventually acquired a Spanish land grant to the area in 1796. He was a close friend and "neighbor" of Denis Julien, although situated some 165 miles to the north. They were both *Québeçois*, and when he traveled upriver to Mackinac, Julien would often stop at *La Mine*, while Dubuque, when he transported his lead downriver to St. Louis, would often stop at the Des Moines Rapids.

According to pre-trial depositions given by Joseph Collin, in the years 1807, 1808, and 1809, Dubuque gave memorandums, or orders, to Julien for merchandise to be purchased by him while at Mackinac. Julien would then deliver the goods to Dubuque while on his way back to Head of Rapids. Sometimes Dubuque would pay Julien upon delivery, sometimes not. In November of 1809, Julien sent Collin on ahead with the merchandise obtained that fall for Dubuque, the cost of which was 2,400 *livres*, or approximately 750 U.S. dollars. Dubuque evidently paid some 400 *livres* of his account, and wrote out a promissory note for the remaining 2,000.

Joseph Collin served in the capacity of clerk for Denis Julien from 1807 until 1809. He was another of the French-Canadians who sometimes went by a *dit* (an additional name), in his case, Laliberté. La Liberté was the name given by François Cailhol in 1798 to one of Julien's five companions traveling in a canoe downstream to St. Louis. Similar to Joseph Marie in 1806, who was from nearby St. Charles, Collin was from St. Louis. It seems that while Julien may have customarily hired his *engagés* from up in Mackinac, his clerks, or seconds-in-command, were from the St. Louis area.

Once again it is informative to note what items were paid for by Dubuque in 1809: fourteen deerskins left at Prairie du Chien, 49 *livre*; forty-one pounds of flour and bags, 30 *livre*; two pounds of grease, 3 *livre*; one pound of powder, 10 *livre*; four pounds of shot, 8 *livre*; two dozen knives, 36 *livre*; one fine hat, 48 *livre*; six [twists] of tobacco, 19 *livre*; one pipe, 10 *livre*; one trunk, 90 *livre*; and one large silver spoon, 84 *livre*.

Sometime later, while returning from St. Louis back upriver to his home, Dubuque suddenly became seriously ill and stayed the rest of the winter of 1809-10 at Denis Julien's house at Head of Rapids.[4] During his convalescence there, Joseph Collin testified that he heard Dubuque say that he was in debt to Julien to the amount of $250 to $300. With the coming of spring Dubuque was able to continue on up the Mississippi to his own home, but died soon thereafter on March 24. His death has been attributed to either lead poisoning, from his many years of mining, or perhaps tuberculosis and/or pneumonia. Soon after Dubuque's death, on May 25 Julien put in a claim to Pierre Chouteau, who in Dubuque's last weeks had been assisting him at his mines. The claim was for $435.16, but was turned down on the grounds that the estate was insolvent.

After repeated requests for reimbursement were ignored, Julien finally filed suit against Auguste Chouteau and the Dubuque estate in August, 1813, for a total of $900. The case went to trial during the October Term of the General Court of St. Louis, and the defense pled *non assumpsit*. They could not assume the claimed debt as the estate was insolvent. The jury agreed and rendered a final verdict in favor of the defendants.[5]

Julien's next lawsuit was filed on May 11, 1815. It was actually a joint suit of François Derouin and Denis Julien against Patrick Lee, in a case of *replevin*. They had secured a writ to *repleve*, or repossess, a quantity of furs belonging to them that had been detained by Lee in his warehouse against "sureties and pledges." The furs in question were itemized as: three packs of beaver skins, weighing 328 pounds, valued at $700; twenty-four packs of shaved deerskins, weighing about 2,485 pounds, valued at $1,200; four packs of raccoon skins, valued at $300; and one pack of muskrat and otter skins, valued at $200.

These accumulated furs and pelts were evidently the season's take from the winter of 1814-15. François Derouin (also sometimes spelled Derouen) was a longtime St. Louis fur trader and was probably one of the "three or four" men who accompanied Julien and his son that winter on the Missouri. For the first three decades of the 1800s, Patrick Lee was a St. Louis broker and merchant, heavily involved in the fur trade. From the wording of the suit, he must have advanced Julien and Derouin trade goods for their 1814-15 venture, and upon their return in late spring had held their winter's take until he had been repaid.

The furs were repossessed from the Lee warehouse on May 11 by the St. Louis district sheriff and delivered to François Derouin.[6] Evidently, Julien was not in the area to take charge of the furs himself, and this is probably why Derouin's name appears with his on the original suit. In a case of *replevin* such as this, the appellants, Derouin and Julien, upon having their goods returned, promised to appear in court at a later date if it became necessary. Presumably, however, everything was resolved satisfactorily, as no future court case was convened in the matter.

Where Julien probably was in early May of 1815 was farther to the west along the Missouri River, somewhere in the vicinity of the tiny village of Cote sans Dessein. On April 18, he had delivered goods and supplies there to a contingent of Missouri Rangers, part of the territorial militia. A promise of payment of $138 was made by Jesse Van Bibber, a member of the unit, but was never fulfilled. After continued refusals, Julien finally filed suit against Van Bibber on September 10, 1817, for $250 in damages.

The subsequent case dragged on for over a year. Various delays were extended until November of 1818. Part of the problem was simply the distances involved in the gathering of witnesses for pre-trial depositions. In 1817, Cote sans Dessein was in what was then the county of St. Charles, but was located some ninety miles to the west of the St. Louis area. Three of the witnesses for the plaintiff, Julien, lived there, while two of the three witnesses for the defendant, Van Bibber, lived in small, rural locales outside of St. Charles. Just executing the writs by the district sheriff proved extremely time-consuming.[7]

There was also the matter of Van Bibber himself. Captain Nathan Boone, son of the famed frontiersman, was the actual commander of the Missouri Rangers. Jesse Van Bibber was listed simply as a private in the unit, though it was evidently he that took possession of the goods and supplies at Cote sans Dessein when they were delivered there by Julien. Therefore, part of the delays may have been a question of authority. Was this a civilian matter with Van Bibber, or a governmental matter with the Territory of Missouri? Was Van Bibber actually responsible for a debt that he may have assumed in the name of a governmental military unit?

These questions are never answered, and as far as the court records of the lawsuit show, the case never came to trial. No verdict is listed, and like most of Julien's earlier litigations, it very well may have been settled out-of-court. On May 3, 1819, however, Van Bibber did file a counter-suit against Julien for "damages" in the earlier case. This is, perhaps, an indication that he very well may have received some sort of a favorable ruling earlier, and was now seeking monetary compensation. The sum of $71.06, though, does seem a rather small and surprisingly specific figure. Once again, no verdict is shown in the court records.[8]

The number of judicial cases that Denis Julien was involved in during his fourteen years as an established fur trader, show that he was not the type of businessman to sue at the slightest pretext or take someone to court on a mere whim. In many of the cases where he did eventually file suit it was only after an extended period of time, sometimes over a year, of continual and repeated requests on his part for satisfaction. With Julien's long background as an "in the woods" fur trader with the Native Americans, and among whom he also lived for several years, he was most likely not comfortable in a courtroom setting and only resorted to judicial law as a last resort.

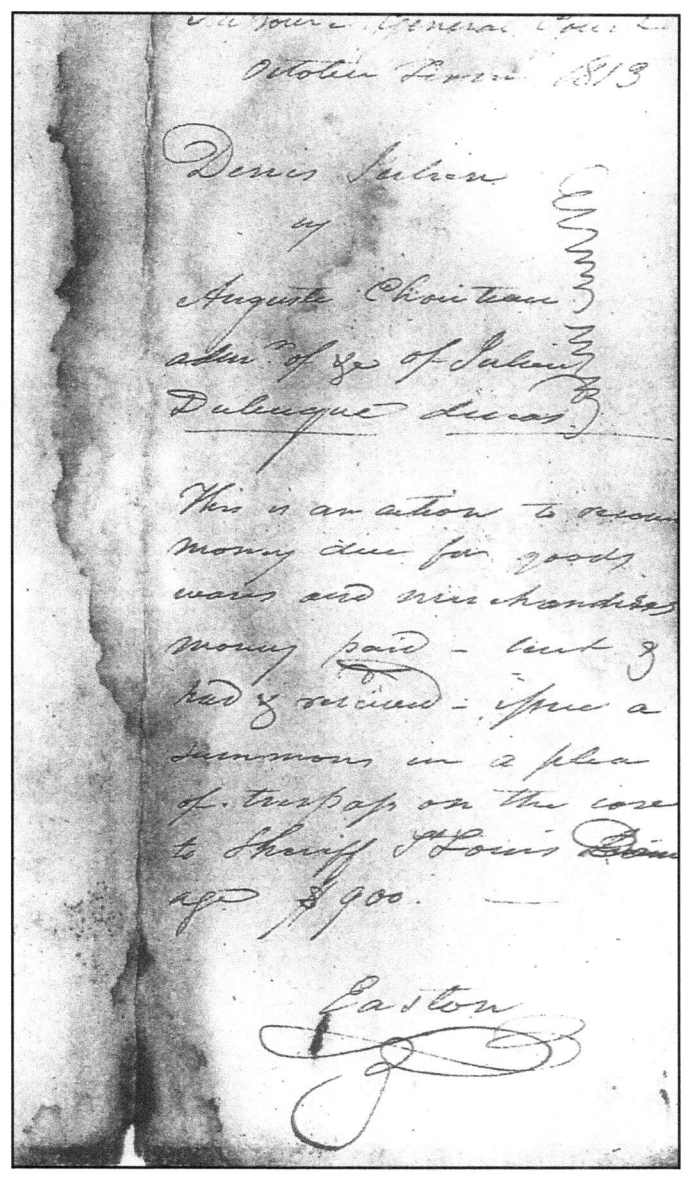

Denis Julien vs Auguste Chouteau, October Term, 1813.
Missouri State Archives
Jefferson City, Missouri.

SIX
PRAIRIE DU CHIEN

John Jacob Astor's giant American Fur Company, headquartered in New York City, would in 1819 make an equally large impact on the life of Denis Julien. The Convention of 1818 in London had finally established the 49th parallel of latitude, extending from the Lake of the Woods in northern Minnesota to the crest of the Rocky Mountains, as the official border between the United States and Canada. As a result, Astor's fur company quickly bought out the various Canadian trading concerns that had been operating in U. S. territory south of that line. He then proceeded to hire hundreds of suddenly unemployed British traders and French *voyageurs* to work for him.

After being rather silent in the fur business during 1818, in mid-February of 1819, Julien applied to Ramsey Crooks, the American Fur Company's field manager, for a supply of trade goods.[1] In his reply on March 19, however, Crooks informed Julien that the company had decided not to "extend" their trade to him and therefore found it impossible to equip his upcoming summer venture.[2] This refusal was actually in no way a personal affront, but was simply Julien's being unluckily caught up in a much larger financial crisis.

For the American Fur Company, its success in the field at this time was not matched by equal monetary profits in the international fur market. In 1819, a financial panic was shaking the eastern United States, and even extended across the Atlantic Ocean to Western Europe. Following the War of 1812, farm goods and foodstuffs saw a dramatic increase as exports, and the ensuing profits encouraged large-scale land speculation. The unregulated issuance of credit by state banks, as well as the national Bank of the United States, fueled a tremendous inflation during these postwar years. However, when demand in Europe eventually slowed, investors in these schemes began to lose money. To try and establish some control, in 1818 the Bank of the United States began to withdraw promissory notes from circulation and required each branch bank to redeem its own notes. By the fall of 1819, some banks and mercantile establishments started to fail, and an economic depression began. The resulting panic led to a steep decline everywhere in the prices for various goods, including furs. Astor, after he had surveyed the dismal fur auction returns in London, ordered Crooks to economize and cut back.

Thus, Julien once again found himself in the wrong place at the wrong time, and his world literally began to change before his eyes. In December of 1818, Illinois Territory, where Julien and his family had lived for over thirteen years, became the state of Illinois. New laws and altered taxation rates may have now been a problem for him. More importantly, the refusal of goods from the American Fur Company the following spring effectively kept him from pursuing his fur trade livelihood. Though he did have his 640 acres of land at the head of the Des Moines Rapids, Julien now found himself in the financial dilemma of being "land rich, but cash poor." Even his longtime trade customers, the Grand River Ioways, could not provide him an economic haven. By the summer of 1819, disagreements with the ever-growing wave of new white settlers to the Missouri Territory forced these Ioways to move yet one more time, northwest to finally join the other bands already located on the Missouri River in the Council Bluffs area.

Therefore, on April 28, 1819, Julien signed a quit claim deed, selling his property to Rufus Easton, a St. Louis lawyer and also a land speculator, for the sum of $320. The description of the property listed a log house, hen house, stable, about ten acres of cultivated land, and a fenced-in garden. The deed was approved by the Northern Circuit Court in St. Louis on May 11, and recorded in Edwardsville, county seat of Madison County, Illinois, on June 23.[3] The land in cultivation, the garden, and the hen house, were all indicative of Julien's home life, or at least his family's, when he was not actually engaged in the various aspects of the fur trade.

Just what transpired with Julien and his family after the April 28 sale of their property is difficult to trace. Six days later, on May 3, he was served a writ by the county sheriff in the town of St. Charles and ordered to appear before the St. Charles Circuit Court on July 5.[4] This was in response to the counter-suit filed against Julien by Jesse Van

Bibber. There is no record that Julien ever appeared before the judge on July 5, and on July 21 a letter to him lay unclaimed at the St. Louis post office.[5] On April 8, 1820, there was yet another unclaimed letter to Julien, this time at the Chariton post office, far to the west in the area where the Grand River Ioway band had lived until the previous year.[6] Indeed, there is no official word of Julien's whereabouts for almost two years, until on March 27, 1821, he was a signee of a petition at Prairie du Chien.

* * *

The history of Prairie du Chien, often mentioned over the years in connection with Denis Julien, was long and varied. The prairie itself was a strip of floodplain running for about ten miles north of the mouth of the Wisconsin River, *Ouisconsin* to the early French, and *Meskonsing*, "red stone place," to the native Algonquin people. Some four miles in width, the land lay between the Mississippi River on the west and a steep, timbered bluff to the east. Some three miles above the Wisconsin, a backwater, or slough, later called the *Marais St. Feriole* by the French, curved through the prairie. Between the slough and the Mississippi was a large, elongated, low mound of ground, which actually formed an island during the high, spring-season water. This traditionally was a longtime favorite meeting place for the surrounding Native American tribes and bands.

French fur trader Nicholas Perrot traveled southwest to the mouth of the Wisconsin in 1673, and at that time may have established Fort St. Nicholas, the so-called "Old French Fort" in what was later termed Lowertown of Prairie du Chien. Tradition has it that some French *coureurs des bois* made the site their headquarters in 1737, when a trading post was built and a stockade erected around the buildings. A French trader, Jean Pierre Cardinal, is usually given credit for being Prairie du Chien's first permanent resident in about 1754. In the fall of 1760, after the defeat of the French military forces at Québec and Montréal a year earlier, it is said that some British army deserters made their way southwest to the village of Prairie du Chien, where they settled down with the handful of French residents already living there. They proceeded to trade with the surrounding natives, and cared little who governed them as long as they could make good money before any sort of official law and order was established in the region.

In 1766, New England trader Jonathan Carver gave the area the first historic designation of Prairie du Chien, French for "Plain of the Dog." While some writers attribute the appellation to the name of the nearby band of Fox Indians, most historians now accept that it came from the name of the Fox chieftain, *Alin*, which meant "Dog." Like Mackinac to the north, but on a somewhat smaller scale, the area around the village was now the scene each year of not only a great gathering of the tribes, but a *rendezvous* for white traders. At this time the natives would bring in their furs and pelts to trade with the Europeans, while the *coureurs des bois* would prepare for their upcoming winter trading ventures.

Even after the Treaty of Paris in 1783 and the Northwest Ordinance of 1787, Prairie du Chien was too far distant from Washington, D.C. to receive much, if any, attention. Whatever informal organization existed remained under the direction of the French and British traders. When Captain Zebulon M. Pike visited the village in 1805, it consisted of eighteen dwellings along two streets, on what was now being called The Island. There were also a few other habitations east of the slough and scattered around the surrounding area. In 1811, Indian Agent Nicholas Boilvin reported that most of the male residents were French-Canadians who had married Indian wives, and either had, or were now, working in some aspect of the fur trade. Following the War of 1812 and the signing of the peace treaties with the various upper Mississippi tribes in 1815, the U.S. government erected Fort Crawford at Prairie du Chien in 1816. At the same time a government trading factory was also established, just a short ways south of the fort.

* * *

Why Denis Julien ended up in Prairie du Chien is not known with any absolute certainty, but circumstances and conditions do suggest a possible reason. While in the Fort Madison area from 1808 until 1813, he worked closely with the U.S. government factor there, John W. Johnson, and was also associated with the resident U.S. Indian Agent, Nicholas Boilvin, from his work with the Ioway tribe. After the construction of Fort Crawford at Prairie du Chien, Boilvin was transferred there, and with the establishment of the new trading factory, Johnson was appointed factor. Therefore, at least two individuals with whom Julien had worked with in the past already resided at Prairie du Chien.

There was also the factor of location and cultural environment. After the War of 1812, that part of the upper Mississippi region around St. Louis, and even upriver as far as northern Illinois and Iowa, had come more and more under the influence of the new American settlers. The old French, or Gallic, way of life was fast disappearing, and both the population and the hustle and bustle of living had increased dramatically. Prairie du Chien, on the other hand, was not only already familiar to Julien, but still retained the bygone *milieu*, or way of life, he was used to – especially that pertaining to the fur trade.

The petition signed by Julien on March 27, 1821, at Prairie du Chien, was from the "inhabitants of Crawford County...." They were petitioning Lewis Cass, Governor of Michigan Territory (of which Wisconsin was then a part), to change the appointed time for the sitting of the county court. The twenty-two signers explained that the scheduled time was when most of the "commercial part of the citizens" were absent from the area.[7] These "commercial citizens" were the fur traders that made up a significant percentage of the population, and the appointed time for the court was when they were away from Prairie du Chien on their annual trading ventures.

There was yet another petition later in 1821, dated December 24, that dealt with the confirmation of land claims. At the session of the United States Congress of 1819-1820, an act was passed to take testimonies concerning private land claims made in U.S. territory by the British government prior to the 1796 exit proviso in the Jay Treaty. Therefore, in 1820 commissioners were sent out by the U.S. government to take such testimonies. Judge Isaac Lee arrived in Prairie du Chien that fall. He called upon witnesses to tell what they knew about each case, and then either confirmed or rejected the claim examined. On his 1820 map is shown eighty-seven such claims, none of which contain Julien's name. While most were confirmed by Lee, over a score were not.

The petition of December 24 was directed to the U.S. Congress from the "inhabitants of Prairie du Chien." The twenty-six signers, which once again included Denis Julien, were citizens whose land claims had not been confirmed by Judge Lee. In this petition they were requesting Congress to confirm these claims, even if they had been made after 1796.[8]

Meanwhile, after several years of lobbying, on May 6, 1822, a bill was passed by Congress which finally abolished the U.S. trading factory system. Private fur companies, led mainly by Astor's American Fur, had maintained that one of the principal intentions of the system was to drive out and lessen the influence of British traders in U.S. territory. But now, they argued, after the successful conclusion of the War of 1812 that was no longer a valid concern. Also, the continued availability of cheap, low-cost trade goods to the Native American tribes by the government factories seriously hampered and undermined legitimate efforts by the American trading companies.

Abolition of the factory system meant a rush of private traders into the more remote parts of the Indian country. Therefore, when the factories were finally eliminated by Congress, merchants once again sent traders into the Iowa country. Five traders in 1822 were issued licenses in St. Louis to trade with the Sacs, the Foxes, and the Ioway in the area between the Mississippi and Missouri Rivers. Significantly, however, Denis Julien was *not* one of these.

It might be somewhat surprising, then, that on August 6, Julien purchased merchandise worth $40 from James H. Lockwood, an employee of the American Fur Company store at Prairie du Chien. The inventory of the items, however, may be enlightening: ten pounds of coffee; twenty pounds of sugar; three yards of red flannel; three yards of India cotton; three yards of cotton shirting; one coarse comb, one ivory; two mock Madras handkerchiefs; two ounces of No. 18 thread; three pairs of cotton half-hose; one blue printed shawl; four skeins of silk; one pair of small scissors; one black silk handkerchief; two pounds of Hyson tea; and one barrel (thirty-three and a half gallons) of whiskey.[9]

With the exception of the barrel of whiskey, this inventory almost looks to be more of a personal "shopping list" of household goods than it does merchandise for a commercial trading venture. Several of the items seem definitely to be of a feminine nature, and could easily have been for Julien's wife, Catherine, and his younger daughter, Marguerite. Notably, except for this presumed assumption, the last actual recorded mention of Julien's family was in the 1819 letter of trade refusal from Ramsey Crooks. At its conclusion he closed with the admonition to offer his "compliments to the family."[10]

What may have happened to Julien's family after this is open to conjecture. In 1822 his eldest daughter, Marie Josephe, would have been 25 years of age and, presumably, no longer with the family. Marguerite, however, would have been only 15 and, more than likely, still at home. The only other mention of Marguerite left to history is in the brief records of Father Felix Van Quickenbourne, parish priest at Florissant, Missouri, near St. Louis. In 1833, during an annual circuit up the Mississippi River to outlying settlements, he baptized the children of Marguerite and husband Charles Gagne at the *métis*, or half-breed, village of Catfish, just south of what is today the town of Dubuque, Iowa.[11]

Son Etienne had been appointed interpreter for the Ioway Indians in the Council Bluffs area by the U. S. Indian Department in 1817.[12] At the beginning of 1819 he joined the expedition of Major Stephen H. Long to ascend and explore the Missouri and Platte Rivers to the latter's source in the Colorado Rockies. Etienne, or Stephen as he is called in the expedition's chronicles, served as both interpreter and hunter for the joint military and scientific party.[13]

The fate of Julien's wife Catherine, however, continues to remain a mystery. In 1822 she was probably somewhere from 44 to 47 years of age, and at some time after that she may have died from some unknown cause. But there is also another possibility.

Instances did come up when, for whatever reason, a white trader, perhaps leaving the country, could no longer stay with his Native American wife. If they had been together for only a relatively short period time, she might simply have been sent back to her native tribe. But if the length of time was of a significant duration, there was an old French custom know as *s'éteindre*, or "turning off." In this case it was arranged that the wife be placed under the care and protection of another white man. This way she could continue to maintain a way of life that was now familiar and to which she had become accustomed, rather than having to face readjustment to a native society she had long been away from.

Prairie du Chien and Fort Crawford, 1829.
Peter L. Scanlon, *Prairie du Chien: French, British, American*
Menasha, Wisconsin: George Banta Publishing Co., 1937.

SEVEN

LA RIVIÉRE PLATTE

As was the case in 1820, the year 1823 is silent about Denis Julien as far as any contemporary historical records are concerned. From his August 6, 1822, purchase of merchandise at the American Fur Company store in Prairie du Chien until April 6, 1824, Julien is not heard from. And where he was on this latter date is in a completely new location – Fort Atkinson, in the Council Bluffs area of Nebraska. Just what may have transpired in those intervening twenty months can only be surmised in light of current events of the time.

The December, 1821, petition signed by Julien and others asking Congress for confirmation of their land claims, was slowly dealt with. By 1823 all but a few of these remaining twenty-six claims had been confirmed. Since no record or deed of ownership of property is now extant for Julien in either Prairie du Chien or Crawford County, his claim must have been one of those that were refused.

If, during his years at Prairie du Chien, Julien may have worked at times for the American Fur Company, then there was more bad news. On April 19, 1823, Astor sent to all his principal traders a stern directive about frugality. But this cost-saving edict also cut into the few benefits enjoyed by the lower-level employees. Wives and children could no longer live at company posts or travel with the fur *brigades* free of charge. Employees could no longer run up bills against the company for supplies purchased while traveling to and from the winter hunting grounds. And they could not carry more than a nominal debt at the company stores. Since most of the *engagés* had but little spare cash available, this order effectively deprived them of many small luxuries, such as tobacco and clay pipes, that helped make their oft-times monotonous lives more endurable.

On the other hand, if Julien had done occasional work for factor John W. Johnson, as he had downriver at Fort Madison, that also came to a halt in 1823. Because of the abolition of the factory system by

Congress the previous year, on June 9 the United States trading factory building at Prairie du Chien, the lot on which it sat, and all of its stock of merchandise, was turned over to the American Fur Company.

There is also the possibility that, at least for a brief time in 1823, Julien may have moved back down south to his old home at the head of the Des Moines Rapids. In 1867, Isaac R. Campbell said that his father-in-law, Captain James White, had purchased from "Julien, a French trader, all of his improvements, [including] an old dilapidated trading house...."[1] In 1884, White's grandson, James W. Campbell, enlarged upon what was now evidently a family story and added that Captain White "agreed with Julian [sic] that he could remain until the country could be settled...."[2] Lastly, another descendant, Lloyd White , stated, "The one-room log cabin built by Dennis [sic] Julien was still standing when White and his family first arrived in Illinois at the Head of the Rapids in 1823... White and his family moved into the Julien cabin until he and his sons began building a new two-story log cabin nearby...."[3]

Land records show that James White did not purchase and actually acquire title to his land at Head of Rapids until August 17, 1826. Furthermore, it was bought from Rufus Easton, not Denis Julien. This is in complete agreement with the quit claim deed purchase of Easton from Julien in 1819. As Julien had done back in 1805, White and his family must have simply "squatted" on the land from their arrival in 1823 until 1826. Much of the time in between they checked upon and evidently satisfied themselves of the legality of the Julien-Easton claim.

Therefore, while there is no contemporary written evidence, it is entirely possible that the Whites did in fact allow Julien to stay with them for at least a short period of time in 1823. In his later article, Lloyd White added, rather significantly, "but during this interval the trading house burned and Julien departed."[4]

In 1823, Denis Julien would have been around 50 years of age. Maybe he was at a stage that we would now refer to as a "mid-life crisis." Perhaps the responsibilities of a family, the pressures of his commercial endeavors, the contentiousness of his various court cases, as well as his recent financial troubles, all contributed to simply wear him down. As one writer has described such a personal state: "It is because they have too much. The more they get, the more they want. The more they have, the more care they must take care of it. And the more they possess, the more they have to lose."

So, after leaving the Des Moines Rapids area, why did Denis Julien end up at Fort Atkinson, Nebraska, by the spring of 1824? The answer is probably a very simple one – familiarity. The Council Bluffs area where the fort was located had traditionally been the far western boundary of the Ioway tribe's winter hunting grounds on the east side of the Missouri River. Elements of the Ioway tribe had lived in the region since the 1700s, and the Grand River Ioway band had just migrated there from Missouri in 1819. Julien himself had frequented the area as a trader since at least the winter of 1801-02, if not before.

And like Fort Crawford at Prairie du Chien, there were white men now living in the area that Julien had known earlier back on the Mississippi River. Benjamin O'Fallon had been the U.S. Indian Agent for the Sioux at Fort Crawford since 1817 and had now held the same position at Fort Atkinson since 1819. O'Fallon had also been captain of the volunteer company in which Julien had enlisted as far back as 1809. Early in 1823 fur trader Jean Pierre Cabanné joined the St. Louis firm of Berthold, Pratte & Chouteau, more commonly known as the French Fur Company. Now renamed Bernard Pratte & Company, that fall Cabanné was put in charge of their post-store on the west side of the Missouri, just half-a-dozen miles south of Fort Atkinson. As with O'Fallon, Julien had known Cabanné for many years, and as recently as 1816 both men had received licenses to trade with the Sac, Fox, and Ioway tribes – Julien on the Missouri, Cabanné on the Mississippi.

* * *

Some 200 miles north of Kawsmouth and the Big Bend of the Missouri River sprawled the broad, sandy mouth of the Platte River. This wide, but shallow stream would become the great fur trade route to the Rocky Mountain West in the years soon to come. The thirty-five miles above its mouth, to what had been named Council Bluff in 1804, had historically been the home and common meeting place of several Native American tribes, among them the Omaha, Otoe, Missouria, and Pawnee. French traders had visited the area since the early 1700s, even before the founding of St. Louis in 1764.

Nebraska, from the Otoe word *ni brasge*, meaning "flat, or shallow water," and referring to the Platte River, was the general name given to the area west of the Missouri River and rolling further across the Great Plains. Much of this western side of the Missouri was bordered by a line of bluffs, which began just a few miles above the mouth of the Platte and undulated northward for some thirty-five miles. The original Council Bluff (singular) at this north end was the meeting place in 1804 between members of the Lewis and Clark expedition and representatives of the Omaha, Otoe, and Pawnee tribes. It was not long, however, before the name (plural) was extended to the whole length of the bluffs to the south.

Fort Atkinson was one of a planned series of United States military posts to be established along the Missouri River, to support the American fur trade and counteract British influence south from Canada onto the northern plains. Colonel Henry Atkinson was in command of the troops which arrived at Council Bluff in September of 1819. Their winter camp, on the bottomland at the foot of the high bluff, was called Cantonment Missouri. The permanent fort, to be built atop the bluff, was begun the following spring.

When Denis Julien arrived at the fort in either late 1823 or early 1824, the location of the installation commanded the Missouri River below. It was made of logs, the barracks in the shape of a quadrangle, with three gates and a bastion, or blockhouse, in two of the angles of the surrounding wall. To the north of the fort was a council house for meetings with the natives, a sawmill, gristmill, and gun shop. To the south were two storehouses. Below the bluff, closer to the edge of the river, were a store, bakery, blacksmith shop, and carpenter's shop. Gardens were located on the river bottom, while corn and wheat fields were planted in the prairie areas to the west. Livestock grazed there, too, the prairie grasses also providing hay for winter feeding.

Cabanné's Post was located about six miles south of Fort Atkinson. Originally established by the Berthold, Pratte & Chouteau Company of St. Louis in 1822, it was then called simply the Otoe Post, after the local native tribe. But in the fall of 1823, after Jean Pierre Cabanné was put it charge, it soon became known as Cabanné's Post. In 1823, it was simply a single log building, or house, but not long after Julien's arrival in the area, the post had grown to a row of buildings, including the original store and new houses for the employees. The southward-extending Council Bluffs rose back of the post, here more rolling hills than actual steep-faced cliffs. Through the center of the post buildings ran a small stream, Ponca Creek, the banks of which were lined by large cottonwood trees. Between the post and the river the bottomland was level and marshy, while above the hills the rolling prairie stretched away to the western horizon.

* * *

Some of Denis Julien's activities at and around Fort Atkinson are known from the diary of James Kennerly, the post's civilian sutler. On April 6, 1824, he delivered three mules to Julien for J. P. Cabanné.[5] About a month later, on May 1, when writing to Bernard Pratte & Company, he mentioned enclosing Julien's "account for salary," which, interestingly enough, was a mere 92 cents.[6] Kennerly is then silent concerning Julien until just after Christmas the next year, 1825. On December 26 he told of a work party under a Lieutenant Nichols that was sent across the Missouri to cut wood. Kennerly then briefly added: "Julian [sic] shot one of Cabanné's men on the side of the face & was brought up, no great harm done."[7]

From these three diary entries, it appears that Julien was doing odd jobs around the fort, just as he had done at Fort Madison, although now on a much smaller scale. He is also mentioned in two of the instances in connection with Jean P. Cabanné. There was much interaction between the military post and the private trading post because of their proximity to one another during the years they co-existed. During the summer of 1825, though not named individually, there were nine French *engagés* and their families employed at Cabanné's Post. Possibly Julien was one of them.

The post-Christmas shooting incident, though regarded as of minor importance to sutler Kennerly, was evidently considered serious enough by the military officials for Julien to be "brought up" on charges. While he was not an actual member of the military, the wood-cutting party, of which he was a part, was under the charge of an Army officer. Also, where there was no established civilian "government," the local military would often assume the role of law enforcement. From this it would seem that the shooting was no mere accident, though no follow-up punishment of any kind is recorded.

However, off the official record, perhaps Julien felt, or was privately told, that new, greener pastures might be the best thing for him. Early the next spring, on March 4, 1826, Kennerly recorded selling a horse to Julien.[8] There is, then, the distinct possibility that he was indeed planning to leave the area.

Here begins, once again, another year-long hiatus of Julien from historical records. He was now somewhere in his early fifties, an age in those times when a man might have considered "slowing down." Yet when Denis Julien is next heard from, in the following spring of 1827, he is not only seemingly still "going strong," but is now located in a completely new territory – some eight hundred miles to the southwest, high in a valley of the Sangre de Cristo Mountains, in the Mexican village of Taos.

Fort Atkinson, ca 1820s.
Col. Virgil Ney, *Fort on the Prairie*
Washington, D.C.: Command Publications, 1978.

EIGHT

LA PROVINCIA DE NUEVO MÉXICO

If the Mexican province of New Mexico was completely new territory to Denis Julien, it was certainly not so to the longtime French regime in North America. French traders had made their way from the Mississippi River valley to Santa Fe as early as the Mallet brothers in 1739, and during the next decade several French trading expeditions reached the provincial capital. But the steadily increasing numbers of *extranjeros* eventually alarmed the New Mexican governor, and after 1752 foreigners were denied entry into the province.

Spain's acquisition in 1762 of what had formerly been French Louisiana west of the Mississippi River changed the ruling government there, and Mexican trade took up once more. This time, though, the inroads were from farther south, from New Orleans and across Texas. It was not until 1792 that expatriate Pierre "Pedro" Vial explored a route between Santa Fe and St. Louis. However, the retroceding of Louisiana back to France and the subsequent purchase of the territory by the United States in 1803 changed the situation yet again.

No longer were French-American traders from St. Louis welcome in Santa Fe. The handful that made the attempt in the next decade and a half were peremptorily imprisoned in Chihuahua and Mexico City. Then, in 1821, rumors began to reach the Mississippi valley that Mexico's long struggle for independence from Spain might actually become a reality. Therefore, in September, William Becknell undertook a potentially huge risk and left Franklin, Missouri, with a pack-train load of trade goods for Santa Fe.

When Becknell arrived in Santa Fe in November he learned that his gamble had, in fact, paid off. The Treaty of Córdoba had been signed on August 24, and Mexico had officially become independent on September 21. His meager amount of goods sold at an unbelievable profit, and not only the ordinary citizens, but also the Mexican officials, welcomed further trade possibilities. Going back to Missouri, Becknell returned again to Santa Fe the following year, this time with covered wagons and a much larger amount of merchandise. The trade with Santa Fe now began in earnest with the commencement of annual trade caravans from Missouri.

The New Mexicans had little or no manufacturing of any kind, and attractive, machine-made goods like broadcloth, muslin, calico, linen, velveteen, and other textiles were in great demand. On his first venture in 1821, Becknell had returned with Mexican blankets, mules and burros, some gold and silver bullion, and "hard specie," Spanish milled silver dollars. By 1823, however, and important to the story of Denis Julien, another Mexican commodity had entered into the bartering and selling – beaver.

This new trade item came at a most opportune time in the fur business. By 1823 much of the beaver of the Mississippi valley and its immediate tributaries had been severely over-trapped during the preceding two centuries. The French-American fur traders of St. Louis had, therefore, for the last twenty years turned their attention more and more to the upper Missouri River. Now, here was another possible source for the coveted pelts. The Mexicans themselves at this time did only a desultory amount of trading for beaver and no trapping whatsoever. Thus, in the summer of 1823 an American, William Parker, received permission from Mexican authorities to lead a small party west to the mountains to trap for themselves. Their success prompted a half-dozen or so similar parties in 1824 to do the same, but they traveled much farther – to the San Juan River in present-day northwest New Mexico, the Gunnison and Grand Rivers in today's western Colorado, and even as far as the Green River in what is now eastern Utah.

This is the point where Denis Julien makes his appearance into the picture. His introduction to the Mexican province of New Mexico can be attributed to a single, over-riding factor – what might simply be called the Robidoux connection.

The first Robidoux had come from France in 1665 to Québec, where he became a *voyageur* for a prominent fur trader. The next three generations of the family lived in the area on the southeast side of the St. Lawrence River across from Montréal. All now had farms, but also continued to be engaged in the fur trade during the winter seasons.

After the conclusion of the French and Indian War, Joseph Robidoux III moved south of the Great Lakes, down to the Illinois Country, around 1770. To get out from under the strict controls and regulations of the new British regime, he soon moved across the Mississippi River to St. Louis, in what was then Spanish Louisiana. There he became a merchant and, like his forebears, engaged in the fur trade. During the 1780s Robidoux was active on the upper Mississippi and Illinois Rivers, and in the 1790s on the lower Missouri. After the Louisiana Purchase he aligned himself with the powerful Chouteau family of St. Louis, and later with John J. Astor of New York, both high-stake players in the fur business. Included in Robidoux's trading realm during this time were the Otoe and Missouria tribes along the Missouri River above the mouth of the Platte.

In the closely-knit fraternity of French fur traders in St. Louis and the upper Mississippi area, it would have been almost impossible for Julien and Robidoux not to have known one another. After Louis Tesson *dit* Honoré abandoned his land claim on the west side of the Mississippi River at the head of the Des Moines Rapids, in 1803 Robidoux bought the old Spanish land grant. This was directly across the river from where Julien soon settled in 1805. All six of Joseph III's sons were born in the St. Louis area and all entered into the fur trade business. The eldest, Joseph IV, upon the death of his father in 1810, became the nominal head of the clan and leader of the family fur business. Even before then, however, he had led trading parties up the Mississippi and had been involved in the trading of merchandise at Mackinac. He must, then, have had various encounters with Denis Julien. Indeed, in 1812, immediately prior to Julien's indictment on smuggling charges, Joseph Robidoux IV had also been arrested for similar activity. Julien even served as a witness at his hearing.[1]

After 1815 and the end of the War of 1812, Robidoux continued to trade with various Native American tribes up the Missouri River, and by 1819 was operating on a seasonal basis in the Council Bluffs area of Nebraska. In 1822 he became manager of the Berthold & Chouteau Company trading facility south of Fort Atkinson. By 1825, however, he had struck out on his own and established a post in the Blacksnake Hills area of northwestern Missouri. There he remained for the rest of his life and in 1843 platted the town of St. Joseph, named after his patron saint.

From his Council Bluff post and later from his Blacksnake Hills store, Joseph began sending out his younger brothers on trading ventures to the new fur market region of the Spanish Southwest, to Santa Fe, New Mexico, and beyond. By 1823 most, if not all, of the Robidoux brothers had traveled there. Antoine Robidoux returned to Fort Atkinson that November, and at the end of December was issued a passport to go back to Santa Fe once again. In February of 1824, this passport was endorsed at the fort for Antoine and a company of sixteen traders. His brothers must have returned to Fort Atkinson later that same year, because at the end of September, François, Louis, and Isadore all had started for Santa Fe. Denis Julien was in the Council Bluffs area by this time, and undoubtedly heard the enthusiastic stories of both profitable trading and the possibilities for beaver in the New Mexico mountains and streams.

The late fall of 1824 found Antoine Robidoux and a party of trappers departing Santa Fe for the far northwest, where they spent the coming winter along the Green River in present-day northeastern Utah in the lower end of the Uintah Basin. By the end of the summer in 1825 he was back at Fort Atkinson with a large amount of furs and extolled the richness of beaver to be found in the region of the upper Green River. Once again, Denis Julien must have given ear to these reports. Less than a month later, François Robidoux left the fort for Santa Fe, and by October he was back in New Mexico with brothers Louis and Michel.

In Santa Fe, François received a *guia*, or license, from the New Mexican governor. Though the permit was officially only for trading purposes, it was also a cover for actual trapping. At this time Mexican law prohibited the trapping of furs by foreigners. The winter of 1825-26 was probably spent in the Uintah Basin area that Antoine Robidoux had found so plentiful with beaver the preceding winter season.

Early in 1826, however, before François and his party returned, there was a radical change of policy in Santa Fe. No longer was a blind eye to be turned toward American trader-trappers, even those with already approved licenses. Therefore, in May of 1826, upon his return to Santa Fe, François had a portion of his furs confiscated by Mexican authorities. Fortuitously, for lack of pack stock to transport all of their bales of fur back to Santa Fe, he and his party had left the larger part of their winter's take under guard in the "Indian country." The remainder of the year was spent in negotiations to have his confiscated furs returned, which they eventually were.

The next January, 1827, François Robidoux was issued another *guia* to visit the "Ute country." In March he and a company of men left the village of Taos, north of Santa Fe, to go in the direction of the land of the Ute Indians to retrieve some *entierros*. Literally meaning "buried goods," these were undoubtedly the furs that had been left behind the previous year. Most notable, however, was the listing of the members of the Robidoux party, obtained by Manuel Martínez, the *alcalde* of Taos. Among the fourteen names was that of "Dionicio Julian" – the Spanish rendering of Denis Julien.[2]

* * *

The last documented date for Julien in the Midwest is at Fort Atkinson, Nebraska, on March 4, 1826. The first documented date for him in the far West is at Taos, New Mexico, in March of 1827. He must have gone west, then, sometime in 1826.

One possibility is that Julien traveled with what had by now become the annual Santa Fe trader caravan. In late May of that year almost one hundred persons left Franklin, Missouri, and started for New Mexico. It was reported that some of them intended to penetrate to the more remote regions and be absent for more than a year. This is exactly what Julien proceeded to do. Another possibility, however, is that he may have accompanied a separate party of traders and trappers that had been dispatched during the summer of 1826 to New Mexico. This group had been sent out by Bernard Pratte & Company of St. Louis, who were the owners of Cabanné's Post at Council Bluffs and with whom Julien had close associations.

Whomever Julien may have traveled west with, they probably made their way over a significant portion of the Santa Fe Trail. Not far to the southwest, in what is now Kansas, Julien must have felt as if he was entering another world. For all of his life he had lived on or close to the broad waters of the Mississippi and Missouri Rivers, with their rich bottomlands and well-timbered banks. Back away from the major streams themselves much of the land was still wooded, only splotched here and there with open prairies. Even the more expansive prairieland that stretched to the west of Council Bluffs was rolling and lush with high grasses.

But after fording the Neosho River in south-central Kansas, the last of the thickly timbered watercourses were left behind. The country beyond was much more open, the few trees to be seen hunched down in shallow, mostly dry draws as if to shelter from the seemingly ceaseless wind which rolled the high grass in waves like the ocean. The change was gradual, but by the crossing of the Arkansas River the increasingly treeless expanse must have seemed somewhat forbidding to someone who had spent his entire life among big trees and along broad rivers. Now the sensation of endless, empty space was complete; the visible world reduced to simple earth and sky. Southwest of the spring-fed trickle of the Cimarron River the landscape became hotter and drier, and the tall grasses of the Kansas prairies gave way to the baked, short-grass stubble of the New Mexico plains.

And what must have been Julien's thoughts when he first saw the tall peaks of the mountains known as the Blood of Christ, because they glowed so red in the setting sun? The nearest geographic features of high elevation that he would have seen prior to that time would have been the so-called Laurentian and Ozark Mountains of Ontario and southeast Missouri. But in comparison they were the mere stumps of formerly tall mountains that were now nothing more than high hills. If Julien and his traveling companions went first to Santa Fe, they went up and over the Sangre de Cristos by way of gently sloping Glorieta Pass and on to the tributaries of the Rio Grande to the west. However, if they made their way directly to Taos, they would have threaded their way through the intervening mountains via the deep and rugged Taos Canyon.

In the early 1820s the old Spanish regulations against trapping by foreigners were still in effect, though the new governor of New Mexico was not against the granting of "trade" licenses – for a substantial fee, of course. Even with such permission, though, the returning traders-trappers were forced to pay exorbitant duties to the Mexican customs officials in Santa Fe. Therefore, many of the Americans began to operate out of Taos, a small mountain village some seventy miles north of the provincial capital. It did not have a customs office and was not as strictly regulated. Smuggling was also utilized, with furs being concealed in caches outside of town, later sneaked out by devious routes, and finally secreted into wagons that were bound for Missouri.

The town of Taos was located toward the east side of the Taos Valley, north of the Rancho de Taos and south of the Native American Taos Pueblo. The area was originally settled by Spanish colonists in the mid-1600s, abandoned during the Pueblo Revolt of 1680, and then not resettled until the early 1700s. Don Fernando de Taos, to use the full name of the village, was named for one of its earliest settlers. During the trading and trapping days of the early 1800s its population varied between 1,000 and 1,500 residents, most of whom resided in low, one or two-story adobe houses, whitewashed to a dazzling brilliance with mica lime.

Taos had long been a trade center with the surrounding Native Americans. In late summer each year a great "fair" was conducted, much like that back in Prairie du Chien on the upper Mississippi River and Michilimackinac on the Great Lakes. This must have been, therefore, at least one familiar feature of the Hispanic territory to newcomer Denis Julien. Here came the Comanches, Kiowas, Pawnees, Utes, and other native tribes of the plains and mountains, observing a truce even during the midst of bitter conflicts. The plains tribes brought buffalo pelts and robes, while those of the mountains brought deerskins and, sometimes, human captives to be sold or exchanged as servant-slaves. The Spanish and Mexican traders brought guns, ammunition, knives, textiles, and the various trinkets and doodads which were the staple of the Indian trade everywhere for centuries. Though the annual Taos fair had diminished in size and importance by the time of Mexican independence from Spain in 1821, after 1823 the French-American traders and trappers began to bring their pelts of beaver fur.

However, Julien was not destined to remain in the Taos area for long. After he returned to Taos and Santa Fe from the 1827 expedition back to the "Ute country" to recover François Robidoux's cached packs of fur, he did probably winter in the Mexican settlements. But the following spring he was off to embark upon a new, seventeen-year long stage of his life.

Don Fernando de Taos, ca 1840s.
Lewis H. Garrard, *Wah-To-Yah and the Taos Trail*
Cincinnati, Ohio: H.W. Derby & Co., 1850.

NINE

EL PLATEAU COLORADO

Just where Julien was embarking to was the region known today as the Colorado Plateau, encompassing parts of present-day northern Arizona, northwest New Mexico, southwest Colorado, and eastern Utah. Though the name as such was not used in an official way until it was bestowed on the physiographic province by U.S. geologist Grove K. Gilbert in 1876, the area was often labeled as "Plateau" on even earlier government survey maps. The name is rather a serendipitous one, as far as Denis Julien is concerned, as the two-word title comes from both the French and Spanish languages. *Plateau* is the French word for "platter," and is indicative of the wide, flat-topped shape of the geographic feature itself, as well as the horizontal position of most of its rock layers. *Colorado* is a Spanish term meaning "reddish-colored," and is descriptive of the predominant hue of the region's rocks.

Julien's "paper trail" in contemporary historical records comes to an abrupt end with *Alcalde* Martínez's 1827 list of *extranjeros*, "foreigners." What we know of the next seventeen years of his life comes from two sources. First are oral histories handed down generation to generation by members of the Native American Utes in the Uintah Basin of northeastern Utah. The second, and from which he is even today familiar to modern river runners on the Green and Colorado, is Julien's seemingly new penchant for carving his name and the date on the canyon walls and rock boulders of the plateau country.

By the mid-1820s brothers Antoine and Louis Robidoux, who maintained residences in Santa Fe, had also established a trading house in less restrictive Taos. In 1828, Antoine is reported have traveled north and established a trading post in the Ute country. Located just west of the confluence of today's Gunnison and Uncompahgre Rivers in western Colorado, it was called Fort Uncompahgre, the Ute word for "red water." When Julien also traveled north in the spring of 1828, it would have been logical for him to have accompanied Robidoux as far as the site of his new post. But while Robidoux halted there and began construction of his fort, Julien continued on westward and northward to his ultimate destination of the Uintah Basin in Utah.

Both Robidoux and Julien followed the old Spanish trading trails which led northwest from the New Mexican settlements to the Ute country around today's Uintah Basin and Utah Lake areas. These regions had been visited by occasional Spanish traders since the second half of the 1700s. Though by the start of the 1800s trading into the Ute country had been officially banned by the Spanish government, clandestine and illegal trading expeditions still managed to wind their way north and west through the mountains to the Ute country.

The easiest and most commonly used route led north from Santa Fe and Taos, up the valley of the Rio Grande River, and into the broad, mountain-girt San Luis Valley in southern Colorado. The towering San Juan Mountains to the northwest were crossed at the low saddle of Cochetopa Pass, the Ute's "Buffalo Gate," where trails on the west side of the continental divide led on to the stream then known as the *Tomichi*, today's Gunnison River. Just west of the present-day town of Delta, Colorado, at a good fording place now known (and spelled) as Roubideau Bottom, Antoine erected his fort-trading post.

The old Spanish trading route continued to follow the banks of the Gunnison and finally reached the *Rio Grande del Norte* of the Spanish, known today as the Colorado River. Here the trail split, one headed westward and eventually north over the Wasatch Mountains to Utah Lake, while the other branched northward over the Tavaputs Plateau into the Uintah Basin. Julien followed up this north branch to the Uintah Basin, where Antoine Robidoux had spent the winter trading for furs in 1824-25.

This once again was new territory for Julien. The higher mountains of western Colorado had been left behind, and the canyon and mesa country of the Colorado Plateau was now at hand. The elevation was lower, the climate drier, and the bare sandstone rock more exposed. The pines, spruce, and firs of the Rockies now gave way to smaller and sparser pinyon and juniper trees, intermingled with sagebrush and other low-moisture plants and bushes. Larger trees, such as cottonwoods, lined only the watercourses.

The Native American and early Spanish trader route left the north bank of what would simply be referred to as the Grand River, threaded its way through the looming face of the Book Cliffs by way of today's Westwater and Hay Canyons, to the summit of the Tavaputs Plateau. There the trail sloped downwards via Main and Willow Creek Canyons to the bank of the Green River. This was the *Rio Verde* of the Spanish, but known to the American fur trappers from the north by its Native American Crow name, the *Seeds-ka-dee*, meaning "prairie hen."

On the opposite bank of the Green, the Uintah Basin stretched out to the west. It is an elongated region, extending some 300 miles in an east-west direction and about 125 miles from north to south. The valley is bounded by the Green River on the east, the gentle slopes of the Tavaputs Plateau to the south, the Wasatch Mountains at its head on the west, and the towering, 13,000-foot peaks of the Uinta Mountains to the north. The principal stream of the basin, the eastward-flowing Duchesne River, is formed by several creeks coming down from the Uinta Mountains.

The Uintah Basin is high desert land, averaging some 7,000 feet in elevation and having a semi-arid climate. Winters can be extremely cold, though in most of the valley itself snowfall is rarely more than a foot or so. Blizzard winds, however, can cause deep drifts in some places. The name Uintah, and its variant Uinta, because of the foibles of map-makers are both used today – Uintah for the basin and Native American Ute band, Uinta for the river and mountains. Both come from the Ute designation *Uwin-tah*, said to mean "land high up."

The Ute name for themselves is *Nuche*, meaning "the People." The term Ute comes from the name of the region they inhabited, *Yut-tah*, "the land of the sun." To the early Spanish this became *Yutta*, and finally, in English, "Utah."

Prior to the arrival of Europeans in the 1600s, the Ute people occupied significant portions of what are today western Colorado and eastern Utah, and ranged even farther afield hunting and trading once they acquired the horse from early Spanish explorers. They were never a unified group with a central leadership, but consisted of several bands separated by natural physical boundaries. They did, however, maintain a loose association with one another.

These bands led a largely nomadic lifestyle. They hunted game, gathered edible and medicinal plants, and moved with the seasons within a specific territory. Spring and summer were the gathering seasons; the women foraged for cactus pods and fruit, and various seeds, roots, and tubers, while the men hunted mostly smaller animals. Fall was the time for the large-game hunts, such as deer and antelope, while winter saw a return to the hunting of small game and also fishing. After the acquisition of the horse, groups gathered in larger villages for longer periods of time, and some of the Ute bands now even included buffalo in their fall hunts.

The Ute band known as the *Uinta-ats* would become the new neighbors of Denis Julien. The Uintah Basin, or valley, was a good area for both hunting and fishing, but there were never large numbers of this band that lived there. Most of the families were fairly independent groups of a few dozen individuals, who resided in brush wickiups or skin tepees in the more fertile areas along the streams that flowed out from the foot of the Uinta Mountains. But the basin was also a travel-route between the Ute bands that lived farther to the west and those to the southeast.

So, what were the intentions of Denis Julien, now at the age of around 55, in this new chapter of his life among the Utes of the Uintah Basin? Perhaps not surprisingly, he was to continue to do what he had been doing for at least the past thirty-five of those years – conduct a trading business with the local natives.

* * *

When Julien entered the Uintah Basin that spring of 1828, he was not alone. According to Ute traditions there were at least two other persons with him, and perhaps as many as "four to six." Those named were William Reed, his young nephew James Reed, and Denis Julien.[1] The elder Reed seems to have been the actual leader of the party. Originally from Kentucky, he had migrated to Missouri by 1799 and subsequently traveled to Santa Fe in 1826, perhaps with that year's annual trade caravan. His nephew, James "Jimmy" Reed, born in Kentucky in October of 1815, had evidently at some point joined his uncle in Missouri. He accompanied him to Santa Fe and then on to the

Uintah Basin. Because of his youthful age, only 12 years old, he was called *Too-pee-chee*, "Small One," by the Utes when he arrived in early 1828.

In the Ute stories there is often included a fourth member of the party, named Auguste Archambault (or Archambeau). In later years, however, his daughter said that he did not arrive in the Uintah Basin until about 1830. Born in August of 1817 in Montréal, Canada, at a very young age he went south to St. Louis, possibly with his parents. From there he ran away from home at the age of 12 (1829 or 1830), and "went to live with the Indians in the mountains." Ute native Mary Reed Harris later stated that her grandfather, William Reed, and Auguste Archambault made several trips back to "the States" for goods to trade with the natives. If that included St. Louis, then it was perhaps on one of these trips that the elder Reed first met Archambault and brought him back west with him, possibly as a companion for his own youthful nephew.

Whatever the circumstances, a post was quickly built for trade with the native *Uinta-ats* band and any other tribesmen that passed through the area. By this time, extensive fur trading and trapping continued in the southern and central Rocky Mountains from Santa Fe and Taos. In 1824 and 1825, American trappers under General William H. Ashley of Missouri had also entered the upper Green River area and northern Rocky Mountains, in what is now southwestern Wyoming. As a general rule, the groups led by and composed mostly of Americans did the actual trapping themselves. On the other hand, those made up primarily of French-Americans, such as the Robidouxs, seemed to have kept to the long-established practice of trading with the natives for their furs.

The new establishment soon became known as the Reed trading post, and later Ute informants remembered a white man they called "Sambo" and another one called "Julie."[2] This was obviously in reference to Auguste Archambault and Denis Julien. The post itself was a single log cabin near a spring of water just north of the fork of Whiterocks Creek and the Uinta River. Here the local Utes were able to trade for their first "iron," meaning items made of steel, such as butcher knives, needles, and guns. Coffee was also mentioned quite often, the natives at first attempting to boil the coffee beans and eat them like regular pinto beans.

In the next couple of years, Julien carved his earliest known inscription, his name and the date, in the Colorado Plateau region. As one historian aptly stated, "Denis Julien wrote a solidly backed biography on the rock of the Colorado River Basin."[3] Located not far back from the banks of the Uinta River about seven miles below the Reed trading post, it was incised, perhaps with a horseshoe nail or metal awl, into the sandstone of a rocky outcropping sometimes today called Face Rock, because of its silhouette. It reads simply, "Denis Julien 1831."[4] What induced Julien to carve his name and the date is not known. While none like it have ever been found back in the Midwest, at least a dozen more such inscriptions have been discovered across the Colorado Plateau.

On September 19, 1831, Antoine Robidoux applied for a license from the New Mexican governor to trade with the natives in the country of the Utes. Later, when he reached manhood, young James Reed married a Ute woman and subsequently spent the latter years of his life at White Rocks. Now known as the town of Whiterocks, Utah, it is located just about a mile northwest of the old Reed trading post. In later interviews Reed said that Robidoux, evidently utilizing his license from the preceding fall and seeing the potential of the trading post, in the spring of 1832 purchased the establishment from William Reed and the other men. The elder Reed then returned to his home state of Kentucky, while James Reed and Archambault, now 16 and 14 years old respectively, evidently stayed on with Robidoux, at least for the time being. Denis Julien, however, may have headed farther west.

In the winter of 1830-31, American traders and trappers William Wolfskill and George C. Yount had led a large party westward from Santa Fe all the way to California. They followed the old Spanish traders' trail past the crossing of the Green River, but instead of turning north toward Utah Lake, they continued westward around the castellated bulge of the San Rafael Swell, then southwest through the high plateaus of central Utah and into what would later be known as the Great Basin. Wolfskill's party then made its way across the dry and parched landscape of southern Nevada and the Mojave Desert, ascended the cold, high Sierra Nevada Mountains, and then proceeded down into the warm and sunny countryside of California to San Bernardino and, eventually, Los Angeles. While Wolfskill, Yount, and a handful of others stayed and settled in California, the rest of the group returned to the New Mexican settlements by the fall of 1831.

Julien undoubtedly heard stories of this new route leading west from the Green River, and perhaps after the sale of the Reed trading post in the spring of 1832 he decided to see it for himself. For several years after the Wolfskill-Yount expedition, there were annual trade caravans between New Mexico and California, and Julien possibly went to California with that of 1832. A newspaperman in the early 1900s, unfortunately without citing any specific source, claimed that he had run across a brief record of "de Julien" [sic] in "the biographical dictionaries," saying that he had gone to California.[5] What is known for a fact is that Julien did travel to at least the eastern slope of the Wasatch Plateau. Years later, in 1875, United States geologist Grove K. Gilbert found a carved inscription, either along present-day Ivie Creek or its tributary Red Creek, up which the Wolfskill-Yount route traversed. It read, "D. Julien 10 Mai 1832."[6]

When Robidoux took over the trading business in the Uintah Basin, he erected new buildings on the opposite side of the spring area from the old Reed post, just a little to the north and on slightly higher ground. This became known as Fort Uintah, which the early trappers and traders pronounced "Winty." The establishment consisted of three log cabins in the shape of three sides of a hollow square or courtyard. They had dirt roofs and floors, with port-holes on the outer faces of the buildings and doors which entered into each of them from the inside. All was surrounded by a log palisade. On one side of the fort was a corral, and some farming was also done in the immediate area. In those days there were some good stands of timber nearby, and game, such as deer, antelope, rabbits, and sage hens, were prevalent.

Not long after his sojourn westwards, Julien probably returned to the new fort and very likely worked for Robidoux. Descriptions of the fort's inhabitants were given by a few travelers who happened to leave written accounts: "Fort Uintah... was occupied by those trappers from Taos...." "Among those living at the fort were several old trappers who had passed fifteen years in the mountains...." "It has a collection of Canadian and Spanish traders and hunters with the usual number of Indian women." While not specifically named, of course, Julien would have fit in with any of these descriptions.

Robidoux stocked Fort Uintah from his trading house in Taos via his Fort Uncompahgre post in western Colorado. The merchandise was brought in on packmules, each animal carrying about 250 pounds of goods. Headed by a guide, the muletrain followed in single file, while the rest of the company, mounted on horseback, brought up the rear. The trail from the Colorado River north to the Green is known, not just by the availability of water and the easiest routes of travel, but by several inscriptions which were carved by some of the early passersby. Julien was not the only one to leave his name and date, and, in fact, it may have been from some of his fellow traders out of Taos that he learned this custom.

Near the southern end of this route, not far north of the Colorado in the canyon of Westwater Creek, is a natural rock shelter and good camping spot. Carved inside is "Antoine Robidoux 13 Novembre 1837." A few miles farther, on the sandstone cliffside near an excellent spring in Hay Canyon, is "D. Julien 183-."[7] Unfortunately the last numeral has been lost to the ravages of time and weathering. Over the summit ridge of the Tavaputs, down in Main Canyon, is another Robidoux inscription, this time left by brother Louis and dated "11 Mai 1841." Farther down the canyon, under a somewhat sheltered rock overhang, is "B[aptiste]. Chalifoux," and "Ant[oine]. Leroux 1835." Nearby, one of the New Mexican traders inscribed his name, "Juan Valdez," along with a date of "8&9 NO 1835."

The most common articles of the trade that was carried on at the Fort Uintah post were horses, beaver, otter, mountain sheep, and elk skins, on the one hand, and firearms, ammunition, knives, awls, tobacco, and beads, on the other. One report stated that in later years large numbers of buffalo hides could also be seen drying in the sun on the surrounding meadow. A sizable amount of trade was also conducted with the white trapping parties that frequented the Big Bear, Green, Grand, and Colorado Rivers, with their numerous tributaries, in search of fur-bearing game. One such party said that they had obtained a small supply of sugar, coffee, dried meat, and even a cow at the fort.

Due to the remoteness of the Rocky Mountain trapping region from sources of supplies, beginning in the summer of 1825, Missourian William Ashley started to bring annual pack trains and eventually wagons of merchandise from St. Louis overland to the mountains. At a predetermined location the mountain men trappers and bands of Native

Americans would meet to sell and trade their season's gathering of furs for factory-made goods, both necessities and luxuries, as well as needed supplies for the upcoming trapping season. In this way Ashley introduced the old French *rendezvous* system to the Rocky Mountains.

This yearly practice continued until about 1840, and during that time most of these rendezvous were held along various western tributaries of the upper Green River, in what is now southwestern Wyoming. During Julien's years at the Reed trading post and later at Fort Uintah, they were consistently located along Horse Creek near present-day Daniel, Wyoming. Like Michilimackinac and Prairie du Chien in the earlier years of his life, the ten-day to two week-long mountain rendezvous were times of high revelry; drinking, gambling, carousing, and, perhaps most importantly, visiting and sharing news. Who had been "rubbed out," or killed? Who still "had his hair," or was yet alive? How were beaver prices in St. Louis? Surely Julien, Robidoux, and others at the Uintah post-fort would not have missed the opportunity to attend such a gettogether.

From 1824 until the first part of the 1830s, the American trappers from the northeast and the New Mexican-based traders and trappers from the southeast, did almost too good of a job in harvesting the beaver population of the region. As early as the 1833 rendezvous, one of the St. Louis traders observed that some of the trappers were thinking about moving to another section of the country. There was reported to be a large tract of land lying far to the southwest which was said to abound with beaver. This could have been the canyon country of the Colorado Plateau.

This canyon region was completely different from the Tavaputs Plateau, Uintah Basin, or even the Wasatch Plateau to the west. Though technically a part of the larger Colorado Plateau physiographic province, this canyonlands section was characterized by deep, sheer-walled gorges cut down through the relatively horizontal sandstone, limestone, and shale rock layers of the surrounding plateaus. Along the Green and Colorado Rivers, these trough-like canyons were anywhere from 1,000 to 2,000 feet in depth, while their tributaries ranged from a couple of hundred to nearly a thousand feet. The two main streams, while not nearly as large volume-wise as the Mississippi or the Missouri, because of their steeper gradient did flow with a strong current.

An employee of John J. Astor's American Fur Company, Warren A. Ferris, roamed the mountainous regions of the upper Green River from 1830 until 1835. A map produced by him afterward shows the area below the confluence of the Green with the Grand River labeled "Great Chanion [sic] of the Colorado." Though Ferris himself did not visit the canyon country of present-day southeast Utah, he did talk to and get his information from trappers who had. In 1834-35 he and his party wintered on Ashley Creek in the eastern end of the Uintah Basin. Significantly, just before they arrived there, they had spent several days at Fort Uintah.

By at least 1836, Julien himself had entered the depths of the Green and Colorado canyons, perhaps to scout out potential beaver prospects. At least four inscriptions were left there by him. One is located some 600 feet above the bank of the Colorado River, not far below its confluence with the Green. It appears to have been hastily scratched into the side of a large rock boulder and reads, "Denis Jul---," with a year date of "1836." Because of the spacing between his name and the date, at one time there was probably a day and month given also, but those have now been weathered away. The location of the inscription site is an unusual one, but is adjacent to a long-used Native American trail leading out of the canyon to the rim high above. The spot would have provided Julien with an excellent view for about two miles downriver and overlooking the first three rapids of Cataract Canyon, Ferris' "Great Chanion of the Colorado." Another inscription, some thirty miles on downstream near the foot of the canyon, reads simply, "D. Julien 1836." This would seem to indicate that he did in fact make it through the treacherous whitewater of Cataract Canyon.[8]

The other two inscriptions are found along the banks of the Green River, in what is today known as Labyrinth Canyon. The first is located some 200 yards back from the river. It reads, "D. Julien 1836 3 Mai." The next is found almost twenty miles farther upstream, just a few feet from the river's edge, and is dated, "16 Mai." This would mean that Julien took thirteen days to travel some twenty miles up the river. This is not altogether unreasonable, considering that he would have been traveling against the current and was also likely scouting out the possibilities for beaver trapping.

At the "3 Mai" Labyrinth Canyon inscription, just inside the mouth of the side-canyon called Hell Roaring, immediately next to Julien's name and date is a crude carving of what appears to be a boat, with a straight vertical line extending upward from its bottom. This has been interpreted by researchers and modern-day river runners to represent either a mast for a sail or a so-called setting pole. Either or both would have aided Julien in making his way upcanyon utilizing the upstream eddies of the river current.[9] Just below this etching is what appears to be a "winged sun," but which has been identified by Ute informants as a male prairie hen, flying straight toward the observer. Therefore, it has been surmised by some historians that perhaps Julien was traveling with a Ute companion.[10]

Contrary to common belief, the rivers and streams of the semi-desert canyon and plateau region were good trapping fields, not just for beaver, but otter and muskrats as well. The popular idea of beaver habitat being along fairly small, rushing streams, where the animals both feed on and use the bordering aspen and other trees to construct dams and build lodges, is certainly accurate as far as the mountains and higher elevations are concerned. But the larger rivers, such as the Green and Colorado, also supported a significant beaver population. Here they do not build dams, and their lodges are either on the thickly vegetated banks among the willows and cottonwoods, or are dug burrow-like into the banks themselves. The pelts of the beaver in the more arid canyonlands were inferior to those trapped farther north, being thinner and lighter in color. But they still commanded good prices back east. At this time a pack of pelts weighing close to a hundred pounds was worth around $500 on the St. Louis market.

After his 1836 venture south into the canyonlands, Julien continued to remain around the Uintah Basin region. His next carved inscription is found in the upper part of the Green River's Whirlpool Canyon, not far below what was known to the trappers as Pat's Hole – the Echo Park of today. The nearby inscription, located close to the bank of the river, consists of the initials "D.J." and the year date of "1838." Though his name is not spelled out, the carving is undoubtedly that of Denis Julien, as the capital letters "D" and "J" and the numerals of the date, are made in the exact same fashion and style as his other full name inscriptions.[11]

Fort Uintah, ca 1830's.
Courtesy of Utah State Historical Society
Salt Lake City, Utah.

TEN

UINTA-ATS REVENGE

Life at Antoine Robidoux's Fort Uintah seems to have degenerated over the years. By the early part of the 1840s descriptions left by passing travelers, as well as stories handed down by the local Utes, portray a rather bleak picture of conditions at the trading post. In a journal account written in the fall of 1842, it was stated that the party's stay at the fort was prolonged by some ten days. This was time enough to observe that much of the inhabitants' pastime was occupied in gambling, horse-racing, and "other like amusements."

Though this does not seem to be particularly offensive, a diary entry penned by a shocked Methodist minister earlier in the summer of the same year was much darker. After an eighteen-day wait for a guide, the reverend was compelled to write that the delay was very disagreeable to him on account of the wickedness of the people, the drunkenness and the swearing, and the debauchery of the men among the Indian women. They would even buy and sell the native females to one another. He also said that Robidoux had collected several of the Indian squaws and young Indian boys and girls to take to New Mexico, where the "Spaniards" would buy them as servants. The reverend concluded by unequivocally stating, "This place is equal to any I ever saw for wickedness and idleness."

Whether it was simple greed or an attempt to salvage a failing business, local *Uinta-at* oral histories reveal that the Utes eventually became more and more unhappy with Robidoux's trading methods. One ruse used early on was to trade a rifle for a stack of beaver skins as high as the rifle was long. Often used, therefore, were cheaply-made "trade rifles," the barrels of which were some eight to twelve inches longer than that of a regular manufactured rifle, and so brought in extra pelts. Alcoholic liquor was also long used to "sweeten" trading deals, and in later years it was said that Robidoux began to provide his native customers with large amounts of *aguardiente*, the "fiery water" of the

Mexicans. Finally, and perhaps the *pièce de résistance*, he began to send his own men out to trap beaver instead of buying the pelts from the natives themselves. While this economically cut out the "middle man," it also effectively left the neighboring Utes with no bargaining power and no way to obtain needed goods from the post.

Not just between the *Uinta-ats* and Robidoux, but between a majority of the various Ute bands and New Mexicans as a whole, relationships continued to deteriorate. In the fall of 1843, Governor Manuel Armijo authorized a company of volunteers to invade the territory of the Navajo tribe, who were at that time at war with the New Mexicans. Their raid, however, was unsuccessful. But during their return to Santa Fe, they came upon a band of friendly Utes and, evidently in frustration, attacked them. The Mexicans killed ten of the natives, took three others captive, and also drove off their horses. Tension, fear, and mistrust quickly escalated during the following year.

Conditions came to a head on September 8, 1844. Six Ute headmen and some one hundred braves had arrived in Santa Fe the previous afternoon, and demanded to see the New Mexican governor. On the morning of the 8th, the six headmen were admitted to Governor Armijo's office for a conference. The Utes wanted retribution for the previous year's unwarranted attack, and an increasingly heated argument ensued. Finally, Armijo knocked one of the Utes to the floor, accidentally killing him in the fall. During the subsequent melee, seven braves were killed before the rest finally retreated to the mountains. As a consequence, hostilities between the two groups began almost immediately thereafter.

Sometime in late September or early October, Utes attacked both of Antoine Robidoux's trading post forts. According to Robidoux, who was away at the time, the local Utes attacked his Fort Uncompahgre for the purpose of killing any Mexicans to be found there. Three Mexicans were slain, and the one American present was spared and sent west to Fort Uintah to warn the Americans there. Even contemporary accounts at the time contradict one another, but it seems that ultimately both of Robidoux's trading facilities were burned to the ground by the Utes.

Even today the local *Uinta-ats* regard Robidoux as a symbol of cruelty and deviousness. Robidoux was probably fortunate that he was not at either establishment during the attacks. One account placed him up north at Jim Bridger's trading post on the north side of the Uinta Mountains, while another said that he was back in St. Louis. Either way he lived to see another day. And so, too, evidently, did Denis Julien. One story stated that at the time of the attack, Fort Uintah had very few of its usual inhabitants present, many having already departed because of the increasing tensions with the neighboring *Uinta-ats*. Julien may very well have been one of these.

Far to the south, in the Devils Garden section of present-day Arches National Park, is the last known Julien inscription. It has been scratched into the dark, desert-varnished side of a tall sandstone fin and reads, "Denis Julien 9 6me 1844." The "6me" is the French equivalent of 6th in English, sixth in French being *sixième*. The preceding numeral "9" is representative of the ninth month, September.[1]

If Julien traveled south from Fort Uintah to Taos or Santa Fe, after leaving the Tavaputs Plateau and Book Cliffs he would have had a choice of possible routes. One would have been to head east and then south by way of Fort Uncompahgre and Cochetopa Pass to the upper Rio Grande. The other would be to continue in a southwesterly direction toward the Spanish Trail crossing of the Colorado River near the modern town of Moab, Utah. The location of his 1844 inscription indicates this latter route.

But Denis Julien had not reached his early 70s by being careless in possibly hostile territory. He was undoubtedly aware that a band of the Sheberetch Utes, who lived mostly in today's Spanish Valley-La Sal Mountain area of eastern Utah, commonly camped near the Colorado River crossing to collect "tribute" for the safe passage of American or Mexican trading parties. With bad feelings running high even before the unfortunate incident in Santa Fe, Julien would have wanted to avoid any chance encounters with Ute natives. Therefore, some twenty miles north of the crossing, he would have had yet another choice of trails to follow.

While the main route of the so-called Spanish Trail led south to the usual river crossing, another branched off to the southeast down present-day Salt Valley. It then led up the smaller Cache Valley and finally down a steep, little-used trail that crossed the Colorado several miles upstream from the principal crossing. The wily Julien, veteran of many years among the Native Americans, chose this route of travel. Still exercising caution, Julien made his night's camp up and over the bordering cliffs of the valley, about a mile away from the trail itself. There, in the shelter of a towering sandstone wall, down in a hollow of sand dunes among some pinyon and juniper trees, he left his name and the date.

This seems to be the last definite notice that history has of the existence of Denis Julien.

* * *

While the following is not a description of Julien himself, it may provide an insight into how he might have lived his last years in the Uintah Basin. It was written in 1849 by a traveler on the north side of the Uinta Mountains near today's Utah-Wyoming border:

"In less than two hours we entered the camp of the traders... and found one man... from Illinois, who could speak English. He had two wives (squaws) and several children which he claimed, but some of them were quite dark. His name was 'John Smith,' not a very uncommon one. He was a very clever man, about 35 years old, was not a Mormon, but had taken the women in order to become popular with the Indians and to improve his opportunities for trade....

"All of the other white men with Smith were French, and all had plenty of wives and numerous slaves (servants). The wives were not slaves, but they had slaves all around them. The whole group traveled about and lived much as the Indian bands did, only much better, for they lived by trading while the others lived by hunting and fishing.... At the end of three days after my arrival here a caravan was ready to start to Fort Bridger for winter supplies for the traders....

"Smith was a... man [of] some cultivation and apparent refinement, and treated his women and children well. He said he had been to his old home in Illinois since he had entered upon this kind of life, but was not contented there and soon returned to his Indian friends...."[2]

Thus it probably was for much of Denis Julien's life. He seems not to have been content to stay in his homeland around the head of the Des Moines Rapids, but continued to follow his friends and acquaintances, to Prairie du Chien, to the Platte River, to Taos, and finally to the Uintah Basin. He was a true *coureur des bois*, a "runner of the woods."

Denis Julien, 1844.
Courtesy of Pete Plastow
Moab, Utah.

DÉNOUEMENT

So what did transpire with Denis Julien after September 6, 1844?

Following the destruction of Forts Uintah and Uncompahgre, Antoine Robidoux soon moved back to his older brother's trading post on the Missouri River. Young James Reed, then in his mid-twenties, had left Fort Uintah and moved north to the upper Green River region sometime in the late 1830s. During the first part of June, 1844, Auguste Archambault had been hired at Fort Uintah by Captain John C. Fremont to accompany his exploring expedition to the west.

In 1843, Antoine's brother, Louis Robidoux, had traveled to southern California to look over potential prospects there, and subsequently purchased land at San Gregorio and San Jacinto. He returned to Santa Fe in the spring of 1844 to close his various business affairs and begin preparations for his family's departure. In November they left with the annual fall caravan. This brings to mind the 1938 Denver newspaperman who made the unsubstantiated claim that "de Julien" not only traveled to California, but died there.[1] Perhaps, then, Julien may have accompanied the Louis Robidoux family in their move.

There is, though, no evidence or proof of any kind for this possible scenario. The list of the names of the 1844 fall caravan has, unfortunately, been partially destroyed, but what remains does not list Julien. Modern day historians have been unable to locate him in any sort of California directories now in existence, contrary to the 1938 newspaper statement. Indeed, research has turned up no mention whatsoever of Denis Julien ever being in, much less dying in, California.

However, one other tantalizing, but also frustrating, clue has come to light. In 1937, Dr. Peter L. Scanlan, historian and author, published his definitive history of Prairie de Chien, Wisconsin. In it is a brief paragraph which tells of British trader Thomas G. Anderson's encounter with Denis Julien on the Des Moines River during the winter of 1801-02. In a footnote at the bottom of the page, Dr. Scanlan tersely states: "Denis Julien *died at Prairie du Chien* a number of years later."[2]

[author's emphasis] That is all. No citation; no source for this vital piece of information.

Recent searches have been made of the papers of Dr. Scanlan, now archived at the University of Wisconsin-Platteville. Especially scrutinized was the box of research notes for his Prairie du Chien history. While there were a handful of brief mentions of Julien, nothing was found about his dying there. Additional searches of the marked graves in the St. Gabriel Catholic Church Cemetery in Prairie du Chien and of the St. Gabriel Parish death and burial records, likewise failed to reveal any mention of Julien.

Peter Scanlan was apparently the first to conclude that Denis Julien returned to Prairie du Chien and subsequently died there. Dr. Scanlan was known to be a meticulously thorough researcher, and although he offers no specific reference, the inclination is to take his word on Julien's death.

* * *

One can picture Julien guardedly making his way back alone to Taos and Santa Fe. Fort Uintah, his "home" for the last seventeen years, was now but a pile of charred ruins. None of his original friends or acquaintances in either the province of New Mexico or the Ute country remained. Even the beaver trade had fallen off, hats made from silk now being all the fashion back East and in Europe. He was now likely in his early seventies. Maybe it was finally time to head back home – to the Midwest, the Mississippi River, and Prairie du Chien. Possibly he had friends, or even relations, that still lived around there.

Perhaps Julien spent these last days sitting beneath the rustling leaves of a sheltering sycamore tree, in the gloaming of the coming twilight, gazing out over the *Marais St. Feriole* and The Island to the languid, sun-dappled waters of the Mississippi beyond. Quietly humming an old French *chanson*, maybe he fondly recalled his early days on that river, his life with the Ioways, and of his wife Catherine. And he might have thought back to his more recent, exciting times in the far, sundrenched Southwest.

Upon his death he may have been laid to rest in an unmarked grave, tucked away in a far corner of the St. Gabriel burial yard. Or perhaps he occupies an unused plot belonging to a sympathetic friend. Either way, may you rest in peace Denis Julien.

Au revoir et Adieu.

St. Gabriel church cemetery, Prairie du Chien.
Photo by author.

ENDNOTES

Ouverture

1. Abraham P. Nasatir. "Anglo-Spanish Rivalry in the Iowa Country 1797-1798." *The Iowa Journal of History and Politics*. July, 1930 (28:3). 384-85.

Chapter One

1. Charles Kelly. "The Mysterious 'D. Julien.'" *Utah Historical Quarterly*. July, 1933 (6:3). 83.
2. Anonymous. "St. Louis Archdiocesan Parish Records, Old Cathedral." St. Louis: Missouri Historical Society. Item No. 11, Microfilm Roll No. 171. 89.

Chapter Two

1. Denis Julien. "Certificate, 2 April 1800." *Native Americans Collection, 1694-1998*. St. Louis: Missouri Historical Society. Box 1, folder 3.
2. Anonymous. "St. Louis Archdiocesan Parish Records." 116.
3. Ibid. 142.
4. Lyman C. Draper, ed. "Narrative of Capt. Thomas G. Anderson." *Collections of the State Historical Society of Wisconsin*. Volume IX, 1882. 151-52.
5. Auguste Chouteau. "Transaction: Denis Julien, June 4, 1804." *Fur Trade Ledgers*. Book 3. St. Louis: Missouri Historical Society. 1.
6. Henry Munroe Fisher. "Deposition: May 6, 1805." *J. A. Wilkinson Papers*. Volume II. Chicago, Illinois: Chicago Historical Society.
7. Hancock County Historical Society. *Families of Hancock County, Illinois: A Biographical History*. Salt Lake City: Family Heritage Publishers, 2004. 513.
8. James W. Campbell. *Report of the Organization and First Reunion of the Tri-State Old Settler's Association, of Illinois, Missouri, and Iowa*. Keokuk, Iowa: Tri-State Printing Company, 1884. 35.

Chapter Three

1. Joseph Howard. "Contract: Joseph Marie and Denis Julien, October 21, 1805." *Chouteau Family Papers*. St. Louis: Missouri Historical Society.
2. Ibid.
3. Maryhelen Wilson. *Catholic Baptisms, St. Louis, Missouri, 1765-1840*. St. Louis: St. Louis Genealogical Society, 1982. 53.
4. Antoine Soulard. "Transaction: Denis Julien, May 26, 1807." *Fur Trade Ledgers*. Book 3. St. Louis: Missouri Historical Society. 14.
5. Samuel Abbott. "Mackinac Notary Book, 1806-1818." Lansing: Historical Society of Michigan.
6. Ibid.
7. Thomas Maitland Marshall, ed. *The Life and Papers of Frederick Bates*. Volume I. St. Louis: Missouri Historical Society, 1926. 203.
8. Abbott. "Mackinac Notary Book."
9. Missouri Territorial Superior Court. "Denis Julien vs. Auguste Chouteau and Julien Dubuque." *Case Files*. Box 38, folder 7. Missouri State Archives: Jefferson City, Missouri.
10. John W. Johnson. "Receipt: March 27, 1809." *Fort Madison Factory File*. Record Group 75. National Archives & Records Administration: Washington, D.C.
11. Ibid.
12. Anonymous. "St. Louis Archdiocese Parish Records, Old Cathedral." St. Lou Missouri Historical Society. Microfilm Roll 175, Item No. 8. 144.
13. Johnson. "Receipt: March 27, 1809."
14. Abbott. "Mackinac Notary Book."
15. Donald Jackson. "Old Fort Madison, 1808-1813." *The Palimpsest*. State Historical Society of Iowa. January, 1953 (39:1). 40.
16. Ibid.
17. Abbott. "Mackinac Notary Book."
18. Marshall. *The Life and Papers of Frederick Bates*. Vol. II. 201.
19. Johnson. "Receipt: March 30, 1811." *Fort Madison Factory File*. Record Group 75. National Archives & Records Administration: Washington, D.C.

20. Antoine Brisbois. "Letter to William Clark, 21 November 1811." *Pierre Chouteau Collection*. St. Louis: Missouri Historical Society.

Chapter Four

1. Clarence Edward Carter, ed. *The Territorial Papers of the United States*. Volume XIV. Washington: Government Printing Office, 1949. 215.
2. Benjamin O'Fallon and J. E. Hunt. "Roster, April 19, 1809." *Pierre Chouteau Collection*. St. Louis: Missouri Historical Society.
3. Thomas M. Marshall. *The Life and Papers of Frederick Bates*. Volume II. 85.
4. Donald Jackson. "A Critic Views Iowa's First Military Post." *Iowa Journal of History*. January, 1960 (58:1). 33.
5. P. Lee. "Items." *The Missouri Gazette* (St. Louis). October 24, 1812. 3.
6. John C. B. Lucas. "Notes on Court Cases." *John C. B. Lucas Papers*. St. Louis: Missouri Historical Society.
7. John Johnson. "Receipt: July 10, 1812." *Fort Madison Factory File*. Record Group 75. National Archives & Records Administration: Washington, D.C.
8. Anonymous. "Attack on Fort Belle-Vue." *The Missouri Gazette* (St. Louis). September 26, 1812. 3.
9. P. Lee. "Items."
10. Asbury Dickins and John W. Fornay, eds. *American State Papers, Public Lands*. Volume VII. Washington: Gales & Seaton, 1860. 782.
11. Lyman C. Draper, ed. "Lawe and Grignon Papers, 1794-1821." *Collections of the State Historical Society of Wisconsin*. Volume X, 1888. 127-28.
12. Denis Julien. "Lost." *The Missouri Gazette* (St. Louis). March 11, 1815. 3.
13. St. Charles Circuit Court. "Denis Julien vs. Jesse Van Bibber." *Court Records, 1817*. Box 17, folder 36. St. Charles County (Missouri) Historical Society.
14. Charles J. Kappler, ed. *Indian Affairs: Laws and Treaties*. Volume II. Washington: Government Printing Office, 1904. 123.

15. General Assembly of the State of Missouri. *Memorial of the State of Missouri, and Documents in Relation to Indian Depredations Upon Citizens of that State.*
Washington: Gales & Seaton, 1826. 73.
16. Carter. *The Territorial Papers.* 191.
17. Charles Gratiot. "Letter to John Jacob Astor, 16 September 1816." *Charles Gratiot Papers.* St. Louis: Missouri Historical Society.
18. Carter. *The Territorial Papers.* 378.

Chapter Five

1. St. Charles Circuit Court. "Dennis [sic] Julien vs. Bazil Hebert." *Court Records, 1808.* Box 5, folder 28. St. Charles County (Missouri) Historical Society.
2. St. Charles Circuit Court. "Dennis [sic] Julien vs. Bazil Hebert, Joseph Papin, & Jean Baptiste Lacroix." *Court Records, 1809.* Box 6, folder 38. St. Charles County (Missouri) Historical Society.
3. St. Charles Circuit Court. "Bazil Hebert vs. Denis Julien." *Court Records, 1809.* Box 6, folder 38. St. Charles County (Missouri) Historical Society.
4. Robert J. Willoughby. *Dubuque on the Mississippi, 1788-1988.* Dubuque, Iowa: Loras College Press, 1987. 97.
5. Missouri Territorial Superior Court. "Denis Julien vs. Auguste Chouteau & Julien Dubuque (deceased)." *Court Records, 1813.* Box 38, folder 7. Jefferson City: Missouri State Archives.
6. St. Louis Circuit Court. "François Derouin & Denis Julien vs. Patrick Lee." *Court Records, 1815.* Case No. 12. St. Louis, Missouri: Office of the Circuit Court Clerk.
7. St. Charles Circuit Court. "Denis Julien vs. Jesse Van Bibber." *Court Records, 1817.* Box 17, folder 36. St. Charles County (Missouri) Historical Society.
8. St. Charles Circuit Court. "Jesse Van Bibber vs. Denis Julien." *Court Records, 1817.* Box 17, folder 36. St. Charles County (Missouri) Historical Society.

Chapter Six

1. Walter B. Douglas. *Manuel Lisa*. New York: Argosy-Antiquarian Ltd., 1964. 189.
2. Ramsey Crooks. "Letter to Dennis [sic] Julien, March 19, 1819." *Fur Trade Ledgers*. Book 2. St. Louis: Missouri Historical Society. 181.
3. Silas Bent. "Quit Claim Deed No. 38. Dennis [sic] Julien to Rufus Eastin [sic], April 28, 1819." *Records of Madison County, Illinois*. Book W. Edwardsville, Illinois: Madison County Courthouse. 83-84.
4. Anthony C. Parmer, Sheriff. "Notice of execution: Denis Julien," St. Charles Circuit Court Records, 1817. Box 17, folder 36. St. Charles County (Missouri) Historical Society.
5. Anonymous. "Letters. St. Louis Post Office." *The Missouri Gazette* (St. Louis). July 14, 1819. 3.
6. Anonymous. "Letters. Chariton Post Office." *The Missouri Gazette* (St. Louis). April 8, 1820. 3.
7. Anonymous. "Petition." *Michigan Pioneer and Historical Collections*. Volume XII. Lansing, Michigan: Thorp & Godfrey, 1888. 586.
8. Clarence Edwin Carter, ed. *The Territorial Papers of the United States*. Volume XI. Washington: Government Printing Office, 1943. 211-13.
9. Maurice Blondeau. "Transaction: Denis Julien, August 6, 1822." *Fur Trade Ledgers*. Book F, p. 21. St. Louis: Missouri Historical Society.
10. Crooks. Letter to Dennis [sic] Julien.
11. M. M. Hoffmann. *Antique Dubuque, 1673-1833*. Dubuque, Iowa: Telegraph-Herald Press, 1930. 203.
12. Clarence Edwin Carter, ed. *The Territorial Papers of the United States*. Volume XV. Washington: Government Printing Office, 1951. 305.
13. Edwin James. *Account of an Expedition from Pittsburgh to the Rocky Mountains, Performed in 1819 and '20*. New York: Readex Microprint Corporation, 1966. 425.

Chapter Seven

1. Isaac R. Campbell. "Recollections of the Early Settlements of Lee County, Iowa." *The Annals of Iowa*. July, 1867. 885.
2. James W. Campbell. "Address of…" In *Report of the Organization and First Reunion of the Tri-State Old Settler's Association of Illinois, Missouri, and Iowa*. Keokuk, Iowa: Tri-State Publishing Comp-any, 1884. 35.
3. Lloyd White. "James White." In *Families of Hancock County, Illinois: A Biographical History*. Salt Lake City: Family Heritage Publishers, 2004. 513.
4. Ibid. 513.
5. Edgar B. Wesley, ed. "Diary of James Kennerly, 1823-1826." *Missouri Historical Society Collections*. Volume VI, 1928-1931. 59.
6. Ibid. 66.
7. Ibid. 92.
8. "James Kennerly, Diary No. 2." Unpublished manuscript. St. Louis: Missouri Historical Society.

Chapter Eight

1. John C. B. Lucas. "Notes on Court Cases." *John C. B. Lucas Papers*. St. Louis: Missouri Historical Society.
2. David J. Weber, ed. *The Extranjeros: Selected Documents from the Mexican Side of The Santa Fe Trail, 1825-1828*. Santa Fe: Stagecoach Press, 1967. 38.

Chapter Nine

1. Mildred Miles Dillman. *Early History of Duchesne County*. Springville, Utah: The Art City Publishing Company, 1948. 69.
2. Milt Jacobs. "First Trading Post." *Salt Lake Tribune*. May 10, 1947.
3. Otis Dock Marston. "Denis Julien." In *The Mountain Men and the Fur Trade of the Far West*. Volume VII. Glendale, California: The Arthur H. Clark Company, 1969. 177.

4. Charles Kelly. "The Mysterious 'D. Julien.'" *Utah Historical Quarterly*. July, 1933 (6:3). 84.
5. Lute Johnson. "Carvings on Wall of River Canyon Are Subject of Debate." *The Denver Post*. October 2, 1938.
6. Charles B. Hunt, ed. *Geology of the Henry Mountains, Utah, as recorded in the notebooks of G. K. Gilbert, 1875-76*. Boulder, Colorado: The Geological Society of America, Inc., 1988. 27.
7. James H. Knipmeyer. "Denis Julien: New Inscription Discovered." *Canyon Legacy*. Winter 2011-2012, Volume 71. 15-17.
8. Knipmeyer. "The Denis Julien Inscriptions." *Utah Historical Quarterly*. Winter, 1996 (64:1). 60-62.
9. Ibid. 57-59.
10. Marston. "Denis Julien." 177.
11. Knipmeyer. "The Denis Julien Inscriptions." 63.

Chapter Ten

1. James H. Knipmeyer. "The Denis Julien Inscriptions." *Utah Historical Quarterly*. Winter, 1996 (64:1). 63-64.
2. William L. Manley. *Death Valley in '49*. San Jose, California: Pacific Tree and Vine Company, 1894. 310-311.

Denoument

1. Lute Johnson. "Carvings on Wall of River Canyon Are Subject of Debate." *The Denver Post*. October 2, 1938.
2. Peter L. Scanlan. *Prairie du Chien: French, British, American*. Menasha, Wisconsin: George Banta Publishing Company, 1937. 84.

BIBLIOGRAPHY

Abbott, Samuel. "Mackinac Notary Book, 1806-1818." Lansing: Historical Society of Michigan.

Anonymous. "Attack on Fort Belle-Vue." *The Missouri Gazette* (St. Louis). September 26, 1812.

Anonymous. "Fort Madison." *Annals of Iowa* (Third Series). April, 1897 (3:1).

Anonymous. "Notices." *The Missouri Gazette* (St. Louis). March 11, 1815.

Anonymous. "Petition." *Michigan Pioneer and Historical Collections.* Volume VII. Lansing: Michigan Pioneer and Historical Society, 1888.

Anonymous. "St. Louis Archdiocesan Parish Records, Old Cathedral." Item No. 11, Microfilm Roll No. 171.

Bent, Silas. "Quit Claim Deed No. 38. Dennis [sic] Julien to Rufus Eastin[sic], April 28, 1819." *Records of Madison County, Illinois.* Book W. Edwardsville, Illinois: Madison County Courthouse.

Blondeau, Maurice. "Transaction: Denis Julien, August 6, 1822." *Fur Trade Ledgers.* Book F. St. Louis: Missouri Historical Society.

Brisbois, Antoine. "Letter to General William Clark, November 21, 1811." *Pierre Chouteau Collection.* St. Louis: Missouri Historical Society.

Campbell, Isaac R. "Recollections of the Early Settlement of Lee County." *The Annals of Iowa.* July, 1867 (5:3). Iowa City: State Historical Society of Iowa.

Campbell, James W. *Report of the Organization and First Reunion of the Tri-State Old Settler's Association, of Illinois, Missouri, and Iowa.* Keokuk, Iowa: Tri-State Printing Company, 1884.

Carter, Clarence Edwin, ed. *The Territorial Papers of the United States.* Volumes XI, XIV, and XV. Washington: Government Printing Office, 1943, 1949, and 1951.

Chouteau, Auguste. "Transaction: Denis Julien, June 4, 1804." *Fur Trade Ledgers.* Book 3. St. Louis: Missouri Historical Society.

Crooks, Ramsey. "Letter to John Jacob Astor, March 19, 1819." *Fur Trade Ledgers.* Book 2. St. Louis: Missouri Historical Society.

Dickins, Asbury, and John W. Fornay, eds. *American State Papers, Public Lands.* Volume VII. Washington: Gates and Seaton, 1860.

Dillman, Mildred Miles, ed. *Early History of Duchesne County.* Springville, Utah: Art City Publishing Company, 1948.

Douglas, Walter B. *Manuel Lisa.* New York: Argosy-Antiquarian Ltd., 1964.

Draper, Lyman Copeland, ed. "Narrative of Capt. Thomas G. Anderson." *Collections of the State Historical Society of Wisconsin.* Volume IX. Madison: State Historical Society of Wisconsin, 1882.
"Lawe and Grignon Papers, 1794-1821." *Collections of the State Historical Society of Wisconsin.* Volume X. Madison: State Historical Society of Wisconsin, 1888.

Fisher, Harry Munroe. "Deposition to Gen. James A. Wilkinson, May 6, 1805." *J.A. Wilkinson Papers.* Volume II. Chicago, Illinois: Chicago Historical Society.

General Assembly of the State of Missouri. *Memorial of the State of Missouri, and Documents In Relation to Indian Depredations Upon Citizens of that State.* Washington: Gates and Seaton, 1826.

Gratiot, Charles. "Letter to John Jacob Astor, September 16, 1816." *Charles Gratiot Papers.* St. Louis: Missouri Historical Society.

Hancock County Historical Society. *Families of Hancock County, Illinois: A Biographical History.* Salt Lake City: Family Heritage Publishers, 2004.

Hoffmann, M. M. *Antique Dubuque, 1673-1833.* Dubuque, Iowa: Telegraph-Herald Press, 1930.

Howard, Joseph. "Contract: Joseph Marie and Denis Julien, 21 October 1805." *Chouteau Family Papers*. St. Louis: Missouri Historical Society.

Hunt, Charles B. *Geology of the Henry Mountains, Utah, as recorded in the notebooks of G.K. Gilbert, 1875-76*. Boulder, Colorado: The Geological Society of America, 1988.

Jackson, Donald. "Old Fort Madison, 1808-1813." *The Palimpsest*. January, 1958 (39:1). Iowa City: State Historical Society of Iowa. "A Critic Views Iowa's First Military Post." *Iowa Journal of History*. January, 1960 (58:1). Iowa City: State Historical Society of Iowa.

Jacob, Milt. "First Trading Post." *Salt Lake Tribune*. May 10, 1947.

James, Edwin. *Account of an Expedition from Pittsburgh to the Rocky Mountains, Performed in 1819 and '20*. New York: Readex Microprint Corporation, 1966.

Julien, Denis. "Certificate, 2 April 1800." *Native Americans Collection, 1694-1998*. St. Louis: Missouri Historical Society. Box 1, folder 3.

Julien, Denis. "Lost." *The Missouri Gazette* (St. Louis). March 11, 1815.

Johnson, John W. "Receipt: March 27, 1809." *Fort Madison Factory File*. Record Group 75. National Archives & Records Administration: Washington, D.C.
"Receipt: March 30, 1811."
"Receipt: July 10, 1812.

Johnson, Lute. "Carvings on Wall of River Canyon are Subject of Debate." *The Denver Post*. October 2, 1938.

Kappler, Charles J., ed. *Indian Affairs: Laws and Treaties*. Volume II. Washington: Government Printing Office, 1904.

Kelly, Charles. "The Mysterious D. Julien." *Utah Historical Quarterly*. July, 1933 (6:3). Salt Lake City: Utah State Historical Society.

Kennerly, James. "Diary No. 2." St. Louis: Missouri Historical Society.

Knipmeyer, James H. "The Denis Julien Inscriptions." *Utah Historical Quarterly*. Winter, 1996 (64:1).
"Denis Julien, Midwestern Fur Trader." *Missouri Historical Review*. April, 2001 (95:3).
"Denis Julien: New Inscription Discovery." *Canyon Legacy*. Winter, 2011-2012 (71).

Lee, P. "Items." *The Missouri Gazette* (St. Louis). October 24, 1812.

Lucas, John C. B. "Notes on Court Cases." *John C. B. Luca Papers*. St. Louis: Missouri Historical Society.

Manley, William L. *Death Valley in '49*. San Jose, California: Pacific Tree and Vine Company, 1894.

Marshall, Thomas Maitland, ed. *The Life and Papers of Frederick Bates*. Volume I & II. St. Louis: Missouri Historical Society, 1926.

Marston, Otis Dock. "Denis Julien." In *The Mountain Men and the Fur Trade of the Far West*. Volume VII. Glendale, California: The Arthur H. Clark Company, 1969.

Missouri Territorial Superior Court. "Denis Julien vs. Auguste Chouteau and Julien Dubuque (deceased)." *Court Records, 1813*. Box 38, folder 7. Jefferson City: Missouri State Archives.

Nasatir, Abraham P. "Anglo-Spanish Rivalry in the Iowa Country 1797-1798." *Iowa Journal of History and Politics*. July, 1930 (28:3). Iowa City: State Historical Society of Iowa.

O'Fallon, Benjamin, and J.E. Hunt. "Roster: Volunteers for military company, April 19, 1809."

Pierre Chouteau Collection. St. Louis: Missouri Historical Society.

Parmer, Anthony C., Sheriff. "Notice of execution: Denis Julien, May 3, 1817." *St. Charles Circuit Court Records, 1817*. Box 17, folder 36. St. Charles County (Missouri) Historical Society.

Scanlan, Peter Lawrence. *Prairie du Chien: French, British, American*. Menasha, Wisconsin: George Banta Publishing Company, 1937.

Soulard, Antoine. "Transaction: Denis Julien, May 26, 1807." *Fur Trade Ledgers*. Book 3. St. Louis: Missouri Historical Society.

St. Charles Circuit Court. "Dennis [sic] Julien vs. Bazil Hebert." *Court Records, 1808.* Box 5, folder 28. St. Charles County (Missouri) Historical Society.
"Dennis [sic] Julien vs. Bazil Hebert, Joseph Papin, and Jean Baptiste Lacroix." *Court Records, 1809.* Box 6, folder 38. Ibid.
"Bazil Hebert vs. Denis Julien." "Denis Julien vs. Jesse Van Bibber." *Court Records, 1817.* Box 17, folder 36. Ibid. Jesse Van Bibber vs. Denis Julien."

St. Louis Circuit Court. "Francois Derouin and Denis Julien vs. Patrick Lee." *Court Records, 1815.* Case No. 12. St. Louis, Missouri: Office of the Circuit Court Clerk.

Weber, David J., ed. *The Extranjeros: Selected Documents from the Mexican Side of the Santa Fe Trail, 1825-1828.* Norman: University of Oklahoma Press, 1970.

Wesley, Edgar B., ed. "Diary of James Kennerly, 1823-1826." *Missouri Historical Society Collections.* Volume VI, 1928-1931. St. Louis: Missouri Historical Society.

White, Lloyd. "James White." In *Families of Hancock County, Illinois: A Biographical History.* Salt Lake City: Family Heritage Publishers, 2004.

Willoughby, Robert J. *Dubuque on the Mississippi, 1788-1988.* Dubuque, Iowa: Loras College Press, 1987.

Wilson, Maryhelen. *Catholic Baptisms, St. Louis, Missouri, 1765-1840.* St. Louis: St. Louis Genealogical Society, 1982.

www.ingramcontent.com/pod-product-compliance
Lightning Source LLC
Chambersburg PA
CBHW070617050426
42450CB00011B/3072